# Laptops FOR DUMMIES®

## QUICK REFERENCE
### 2ND EDITION

## by Corey Sandler

WILEY

Wiley Publishing, Inc.

**Laptops For Dummies® Quick Reference, 2nd Edition**

Published by
**Wiley Publishing, Inc.**
111 River Street
Hoboken, NJ 07030-5774

www.wiley.com

Copyright © 2008 by Wiley Publishing, Inc., Indianapolis, Indiana

Published by Wiley Publishing, Inc., Indianapolis, Indiana

Published simultaneously in Canada

For general information on our other products and services, please contact our Customer Care Department within the U.S. at 800-762-2974, outside the U.S. at 317-572-3993, or fax 317-572-4002.

For technical support, please visit www.wiley.com/techsupport.

Wiley also publishes its books in a variety of electronic formats. Some content that appears in print may not be available in electronic books.

Library of Congress Control Number is available from the publisher.

ISBN: 978-0-470-24056-4

Manufactured in the United States of America

10 9 8 7 6 5 4 3 2 1

WILEY

# About the Author

**Corey Sandler** has written more than 150 books on personal computers, business topics, travel, and sports. A former Gannett Newspapers reporter and columnist, he also worked as an Associated Press correspondent covering business and political beats. One of the pioneers of personal computer journalism, he was an early writer for publications, including *Creative Computing*. He became the first Executive Editor of *PC Magazine* in 1982 at the start of that magazine's meteoric rise. He also was the founding editor of IDG's *Digital News*.

His bestselling books include *Fix Your Own PC, Upgrading & Fixing Laptops For Dummies,* the *Econoguide Travel Book* series, *Watching Baseball* (coauthored with Boston Red Sox star and broadcaster Jerry Remy), and *Henry Hudson Dreams and Obsession*.

Sandler has appeared on NBC's *Today,* CNN, ABC, National Public Radio's *Fresh Air,* and dozens of local radio and television shows, and has been the subject of many newspaper and magazine articles.

He lives with his family on Nantucket island, off the coast of Massachusetts, at the very end of the information superhighway. From his office window, when the fog clears, he can see the microwave tower that carries signals from his keyboard to the mainland 30 miles away.

He has lugged his laptop across the United States and around the world. Recent trips have seen him searching for and sometimes finding WiFi web connections and cell phone signals in Machu Picchu at 14,000 feet in the Peruvian Andes, around Cape Horn at the bottom of South America, in New Zealand and Australia, the Canadian Arctic, and in Svalbard, the northernmost inhabited territory of Europe, within the Arctic Circle at the edge of the North Pole ice pack.

He can be reached through his web sites: www.econoguide.com or www. hudsondreams.com.

# Publisher's Acknowledgments

We're proud of this book; please send us your comments through our online registration form located at www.dummies.com/register/.

Some of the people who helped bring this book to market include the following:

### Acquisitions, Editorial, and Media Development

**Project Editor:** Tonya Maddox Cupp

**Executive Editor:** Greg Croy

**Technical Editor:** Lee Musick

**Editorial Manager:** Jodi Jensen

**Media Development Project Manager:** Laura Moss-Hollister

**Media Development Assistant Project Manager:** Jenny Swisher

**Media Development Assistant Producers:** Angela Denny, Josh Frank, Shawn Patrick, and Kit Malone

**Editorial Assistant:** Amanda Foxworth

**Sr. Editorial Assistant:** Cherie Case

### Composition Services

**Project Coordinator:** Katherine Key

**Layout and Graphics:** Stacie Brooks, Carrie A. Cesavice, Reuben W. Davis, Erin Zeltner

**Proofreaders:** Broccoli Information Management, Laura Albert, David Faust

**Indexer:** Sherry Massey

---

**Publishing and Editorial for Technology Dummies**

  **Richard Swadley,** Vice President and Executive Group Publisher

  **Andy Cummings,** Vice President and Publisher

  **Mary Bednarek,** Executive Acquisitions Director

  **Mary C. Corder,** Editorial Director

**Publishing for Consumer Dummies**

  **Diane Graves Steele,** Vice President and Publisher

**Composition Services**

  **Gerry Fahey,** Vice President of Production Services

  **Debbie Stailey,** Director of Composition Services

# Contents at a Glance

# Table of Contents

# Part 1

# The Laptop Computer

Whatever you call it — laptop, notebook, portable, tablet, or AI — the concept behind its design is to squeeze 25 pounds of stuff into a 5-pound box. In this part, I tell you what's inside that sealed box and show you all the ways you can plug things into a device with more compartments, slots, and connectors per square inch than any other consumer device in your home or office.

## In this part . . .

- ✔ Adding hardware
- ✔ Investigating laptop models
- ✔ Going online
- ✔ Working with files and folders

# Checking Out Basic Hardware

Your laptop is good to go all by itself. Okay, let me amend that slightly: You'll probably want to bring along an AC adapter to recharge the battery or run the machine off wall current. But other than that, when it comes to basic functions, it's all in the box. See Figure 1-1.

**Figure 1-1**

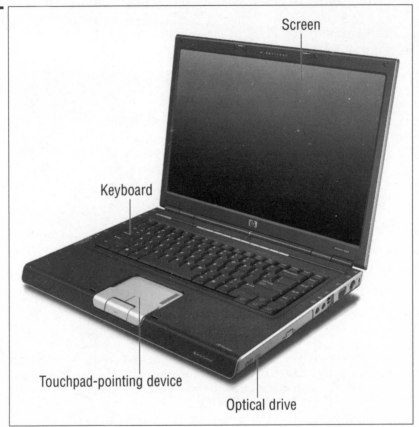

Courtesy of Hewlett-Packard Company

From the beginning of time, or at least laptop time, the box has been built in what designers call a *clamshell* — two main components with a hinge at the back and a latch at the front.

When you slide that latch and open that hinge, you have the following: the upper part, which is the screen (nearly always a variation of a liquid crystal display, better known as an *LCD*), and the lower part, which I call the . . . laptop computer. The upper part may have a few indicator lights, LEDs, or a miniature LCD screen displaying information about its status, and some of the most current machines offer miniature video cameras in the top lip of the frame.

The lower part is where all the action is: the motherboard and its microprocessor, the memory, the hard disk, a CD or DVD drive (on most modern machines), or the latest: a Blu-ray drive (a high-capacity, high-resolution version of a DVD). And because a laptop is, at heart, an everything-in-one-box device, the lower part also includes components ordinarily separated from a standard home or office PC: the keyboard, a pointing device, and a set of tiny speakers.

Take a quick tour of the basic components:

- ✔ **Screen:** Your porthole into the computer. You can read the news, write the Great American Novel, juggle numbers in a spreadsheet or database, wield a digital paintbrush, or sit back and watch a movie, the news, or a baseball game. Virtually all modern laptops use an LCD of one design or another.

- ✔ **Keyboard:** The primary means for entering our own information into the computer, by hunt-and-peck or fast-as-the-wind speed typing. It's not the only way, of course: Many of us get information into our machines from the Internet, from e-mail, from CDs or DVDs, or over a wired or wireless network from another user.

- ✔ **Buttons, lights, and indicators:** What's the point of having all these bells and whistles if you don't have flashing or glowing lights and a passel of special-purpose buttons with unusual icons? There are some that are pretty obvious: on/off and a rotary volume control wheel or a pushbutton that electronically turns the sound up or down, for example. And there are some that must have made sense to some designer some time, but don't seem to have anything to do with any task you ever need to perform.

Here are some indicators you may find on a modern machine:

- ✔ **Power button:** On and off, of course, but also (on many machines) the pathway to Sleep or Standby modes. Many machines also provide one or more indicator lights that tell you whether the laptop is on or asleep, running on power supplied by the AC adapter or the battery, and deliver a report on the power level of the battery. On some machines, a little low-power-draw LCD screen delivers the same information in the form of an icon or text message.

- ✔ **WiFi on/off switch:** Controls the activation of the wireless transmitter and receiver hardware in a modern laptop. You'll also have to instruct the operating system to use the wireless facilities. On most laptops a little indicator light tells you when hardware is powered up.

- ✔ **Multimedia controls:** Yes, it's a serious business machine, even if you catch me watching a DVD of *Airplane* at 35,000 feet over the Atlantic. Many modern machines offer a set of VCR-like buttons to directly control the playback of a video or audio disc in the CD or DVD player.

✔ **Pointing device:** Here's how to give your computer a hand, essentially reaching into the screen to identify, choose, or move text or graphics. On a desktop machine, you might generically call this a mouse, but on a laptop you'll usually find one of the following miniaturized equivalents that don't require additional desk space: a touchpad that responds to the movement of your finger on its surface, a pointing stick embedded in the keyboard that works like a joystick, or a trackball that moves the cursor as you push its suspended marble. (You can also attach a tiny portable mouse to a port on your laptop if you've got the room to use it.)

✔ **Speakers, headphones, and microphones:** Your laptop can talk or sing, or listen to what you have to say. Some models are more oriented toward multimedia than others, but because laptops are often used to make presentations (using PowerPoint, spreadsheet, or graphics programs), nearly all current machines offer capable audio features. The headphone jack, by the way, not only serves to protect the guy in the next seat from having to listen to your soundtrack or the details of your corporate marketing presentation; on most models it can output the sound to a larger, room-sized amplifier and set of speakers.

✔ **Optical drive:** This is a technical way to refer to CD, DVD, and Blu-ray drives, each of which read information by shining a laser onto a spinning disk and detecting tiny dark or light spots, which are converted by the electronics into the 0s and 1s that the computer can work with. Today, optical drives can write discs with your own information, and the most advanced can read, write, and rewrite (erasing old information in the process).

✔ **Expansion and enhancement bays and slots:** As the internal parts of laptops have gotten smaller and smaller, designers have given back some of that space in the form of bays and slots and other forms of pockets that can hold miniaturized expansions of the machine. Nearly every laptop offers the ability to add one or more additional modules of *random access memory (RAM)*. And most allow use of credit-card-size *ExpressCards* or *PC Cards* (an earlier version of the same sort of technology) that can add functions to the machine. Some units include an extra bay that can hold a second battery or a second hard drive.

✔ **Power supply and battery:** The only essential components of a laptop that aren't permanently attached or enclosed in the sealed box are the power supply and the battery. An *AC (alternating current)* power supply takes wall current (modern systems can work with either 110 or 220 volts) and transforms it *DC (direct current)* and reduces it to somewhere in the range of 12 to 20 volts, depending on the machine. That power can be used to directly operate the laptop, which is fine when you're sitting at a desk in an office or your hotel room, but a bit inconvenient if you're flying or driving or sitting out in the woods. The power supply's other use is to charge and recharge a battery that installs in a bay on the side or bottom of the laptop. (You can also run many laptops using a special power adapter that plugs into an automobile's DC output — what used to be called the cigarette lighter — or into a power source offered by some airlines. And some current-model automobiles now offer a 110-volt AC outlet for use with electronic devices.)

✓ **Security lock slot:** Most current laptops include a small attachment point — connected to the internal metal or heavy-duty plastic shell of the machine — for a locking cable. The good news about laptops is that they're easy to move around. The bad news is that bad people out there know this. You can purchase a cable to loop around a pipe or other fixed object; a special lock (keyed or combination) fits into the slot.

✓ **Cooling vents:** The flow of electrons through tiny wires within your laptop is not perfectly free and easy. The friction of the electricity in the pipes generates heat, and the faster the flow, the hotter the temperature. And of course, today's laptops are very fast. Heat within a laptop is exhausted to the outside through the use of vents and one or more fans.

# Cornering Input and Output

I was thinking about calling this section Ports Aplenty, which isn't really a technical term, but nevertheless a pretty appropriate way to think about a laptop. Since the machine's essentially a sealed box meant to travel the globe, clever designers have come up with all sorts of ways to allow you to attach external devices or communicate through wires, networks, pulses of light, or radio waves.

## Current I/O options

As technology marches along, ports may come and ports may go. For example, the versatile USB port has taken over the role formerly played by a number of older means of connection. Designers have ensured that nearly every piece of external equipment, no matter how old, can find a way to communicate with even the most modern machine.

First, consider the ports that are now common on current laptops:

✓ **RGB (monitor) port:** This is an output of the same image seen on the LCD screen, converted to a signal that can display on a standard computer monitor, or on a wall if you use an external video projector.

✓ **S-video port:** This port sends a relatively high-resolution video output to modern TV sets that have a matching input. The picture quality is generally not quite as good as what you see on a computer monitor, but TVs are usually larger than monitors.

✔ **USB port:** This high-speed, highly adaptable port (some laptops offer two or even three of them) can be used for almost any type of device, from printers to external keyboards to various forms of add-on storage. A USB port provides both data and electrical power to attached devices, although some high-demand devices may require their own AC or battery power source. And if you need to plug in more devices than you have USB ports, you can add a *hub* that splits the signal and provides more connecting points.

✔ **eSATA port:** Designers promise to extend the high-speed internal Serial ATA bus from inside the laptop to work with devices outside. Hence the acronym that adds *e* for external. The specification, in its eSATA 3.0 Gbps version, delivers (wait for it) . . . 3.0 Gbps of data transfer, which is very fast—speedier than USB 2.0. In theory, an external hard drive or DVD drive connected this way operates no slower than an internal device. The port also delivers electrical power.

✔ **Ethernet port:** This connects a network interface within the laptop and a wired network of other computers or devices. It can also directly connect to a high-speed broadband modem, such as one that uses a cable television, DSL, or fiber-optics network. The connector, which looks like an over-sized telephone jack, is technically called an *RJ-45.*

✔ **Modem port:** If the laptop has a built-in telephone modem, this port accepts a cable (with an RJ-11 connector) that attaches to the phone network.

✔ **Headphone/speakers jack:** The tiny connector can provide stereo audio to a set of headphones, send a signal to a set of external speakers, or connect to the sound circuitry of a television set, video projector, or stereo amplifier and speaker system. You can purchase adapters that allow just about any audio device to plug into and use the signal from this jack.

✔ **Microphone jack:** Attaching a microphone to this jack permits recording of voice or live music, or provides an input to speech-recognition software for dictation or verbal commands to the computer. The jack isn't intended for use with amplified line signals, such as those that come from a stereo system or an iPod.

✔ **Line-in jack:** This connection, common only on laptops marketed as multimedia devices, allows connection of an external source of audio such as the output of a receiver, a VCR, or a stereo system. If your machine does not have a line-in jack and you want to record amplified sound, your best bet is to purchase a USB adapter that adds an external sound card and additional jacks.

✔ **iLink/FireWire port:** You can call it iLink or you can call it FireWire or you can refer to it by its technical specification, IEEE 1394. Just call it fast. This is a competitive technology to the USB port that Sony (under the iLink designation) has adopted for audiovisual devices including digital video cameras, by Apple (marketing it as FireWire) for a broad range of devices, and by the 1394 Trade Association for anything and anyone.

✔ **Specialized memory slot:** Many modern laptops can directly read from tiny memory cards used in products including digital cameras, music players, PDAs, and cell phones. There is a dizzying array of these cards, including Memory Stick, Secure Digital, SmartMedia, xD Picture Cards, and CompactFlash. For example, Toshiba offers a slot capable of working with many memory devices, calling it a Bridge Media slot; Dell has an 8-in-1 card reader and a 13-in-2 card reader that pretty much cover the waterfront.

✔ **Infrared and WiFi ports:** Technically, these aren't ports since nothing plugs into them from the exterior of the laptop. Instead, these high-speed *transceivers* (transmitter/receiver devices) connect to similarly equipped devices, including standalone printers and keyboards to wireless networks that bring together other laptops, desktops, and Internet gateways.

✔ **Bluetooth and Wireless USB:** Not yet common, these forms of wireless communication are aimed at short-range cord-free communication. Many cell phones use Bluetooth to upload and download address books, digital photographs, ringtones, and other snippets of portable data. Wireless USB transmits data from a laptop to devices including printers, pointing devices, and digital cameras.

## Legacy I/O options

As I've noted, the computer world is constantly changing, adding new technologies and improving on old ones. A bit of overlap is always there: The devices you used last week don't suddenly become unusable this week just because a new and improved way of doing things has been introduced. The industry even has coined terms to deal with this. If a new technology encompasses an older one without making it obsolete, that is called a *downward compatible* specification. (A term that means the same thing, but is not often used by image-conscious marketers is *backward compatible.*)

As an example, USB 2.0, the current specification for that high-speed means of communication, is downwardly compatible with earlier USB 1.1 and 1.0 devices. The older equipment works just as it always did (at the slower original speed), while newer equipment designed for the newer specification performs faster and with new features.

Yet another term is *legacy technologies.* These devices and specifications have been made obsolete by new replacements; in most cases manufacturers continue offering support for these legacy devices for a few years, but eventually that ends. Examples of legacy devices include floppy disk drives, parallel ports, standard serial ports, and dedicated ports for external keyboards and mice. My older laptops still have built-in floppy disk drives and individual mouse, serial, and parallel ports; my newer laptops dispense with all of these connection points, instead advising users to attach old-style devices to the multipurpose USB port or to purchase a special cable that converts a USB signal to a parallel or standard serial connection.

You may find these legacy ports on a laptop:

- ✔ **Parallel port:** Direct connection to older printers and certain other devices that require this sort of cabling in which 16 bits of information march along next to each other in separate wires instead of one behind each other in a serial connection. (Parallel used to be faster than serial, but modern technologies have reversed that trend.)

- ✔ **Serial port:** The original form of computer communication, used mostly for early telephone modems and some printers. Now completely replaced by USB circuitry; if your laptop does not offer this port and you need to emulate an older, slower form of communication, you can purchase a converter than uses the USB port.

- ✔ **Keyboard/mouse port:** The small, circular port used by desktop machines to connect keyboards and mice was also available on some older laptops. There may have been one port for each device, or a single port able to work with either device. Why would you want an external mouse or keyboard when your laptop comes equipped with one of each already? First of all, an external device is usually larger and easier to use. Secondly, you can choose to install a specialty pointing device or keyboard — a board with European accent characters, the slightly different arrangement of keys you find in some parts of the world, or a more precise trackball or optical mouse instead of the pressure-sensitive touchpad or stick used by most laptops. And finally, an external port allows you, in a pinch, to work around the failure of your laptop's keyboard or pointing device.

- ✔ **Docking station/expansion port:** Older machines often were designed with a large connector at the rear that extended the computer's internal bus to an external docking station on a desktop. This was intended to allow addition of more ports, an external mouse or keyboard, external hard disk drives, and other devices. The docking station connector was usually a proprietary design that worked only with a particular manufacturer's combination of laptop and expansion module. Docking stations were not much used by most laptop owners, and have been replaced by the multifunction USB port and by WiFi and wired networks.

# Delving into Basic Software

Okay, here's a metaphysical question: Is a computer a collection of hardware that exists to run software, or is software a set of instructions that is created to make use of the hardware?

And does it really matter?

The second question is the easy one. When it comes down to it, it's the software that gives your computer its personality and the tools you use to do your work. The hardware is very important, but it is just apparatus.

Let me put it another way: If you're buying a new laptop, you should determine what kinds of programs you intend to run on it and then go out and buy hardware that works well with that software.

The software in your laptop includes the following:

- ✔ **The System BIOS:** I've no sooner switched the subject from hardware to software before I must take a half-step back. The *System BIOS* is specialized software that exists in your machine's hardware; its initial purpose is to bring the inanimate chips and circuits and other doodads to life when you press the On button. That is called *booting* the machine, as in "lifting yourself up by your own bootstraps." Its second purpose is to operate the lowest level of the interface between hardware and software: interpreting keystrokes on a keyboard, receiving and moving along clicks from a mouse, and that sort of thing.

- ✔ **The operating system:** This is the all-encompassing personality of the machine, determining the look and response of programs and the way they interact with each other. The most common operating system is one of another version of Microsoft's Windows; as this book goes to press most laptops are delivered with one of the various versions of Windows Vista.

  Although Microsoft would prefer otherwise, the older Windows XP operating system is still very common and popular. As this book goes to press, Microsoft intends to discontinue support for Windows XP effective April 2009. That does not mean that XP will automatically stop working on that date or that you won't find troubleshooting solutions on the Microsoft web site; it does mean that Microsoft will not create new solutions to new problems that may crop up after that time.

  Nipping away in distant third place is the Linux operating system; Linux has a small piece of the server market, a smaller chunk of the desktop pie, and just a few crumbs of laptop cake. (On Apple Macintosh machines, the official operating system is Apple's own Mac OS X Leopard, although most current laptops from Apple can also run Windows as a primary or secondary OS.)

- ✔ **The applications:** Here's where the work gets done.

  - The most popular programs for laptop users include the basic office functions that are part of the Microsoft Office suite of word processing, spreadsheets, and databases. If you're going to make presentations, Microsoft PowerPoint is the tool of choice.

- You need an Internet browser, which can be the nearly ubiquitous Microsoft Internet Explorer or one of several competitors such as Firefox (from Mozilla) or Safari (from Apple).

- Finally, you want an e-mail client and here the choices begin with Microsoft's Outlook Express or Windows Live Mail, or third-party products such as Thunderbird.

✔ **The utilities:** Problems happen. Your hard disk can become fragmented or corrupted. Your machine can catch a virus from a nasty e-mail or an infected piece of software. An unfriendly web site can send a spy to your machine. Windows can become clouded by broken pieces. There's nothing like having the right tool for a repair job, and nothing nearly as annoying as its lack.

# Diving into Laptop Types and Models

All laptops are essentially the same:

✔ On the outside, a screen, a keyboard, and a pointing device

✔ On the inside, a processor, a set of memory chips, and storage (hard drive, CD, DVD, and the like)

✔ In between, a set of ways to get information in and out of the box

The design and the particular combination of very-nice-but-not-always-essential bells and whistles distinguish one laptop from another. If you're looking for an analogy — and who isn't in these troubled days — consider cars. All automobiles have the same basic components: a set of wheels, brakes, steering mechanism, a couple of seats, and an engine to pull (or push, depending on how you want to look at it) the box along the road.

I just checked product listings and reviews on a web site. If I were looking for the least expensive gasoline-powered putt-putt for runs to the grocery store I might consider the oh-so-cute Smart Car *fortwo* model with a list price of about $11,590; it includes in its tiny front end a 70-horsepower three-cylinder engine with seats for a driver and a passenger. In back is just enough space for three or four bags of kettle-cooked salt and vinegar potato chips and a 12-pack of India Pale Ale.

On the other hand, I could dip into petty cash and pick up a pulsating yellow Lamborghini *Murcielago* Roadster, which is anything but cute. Its suggested price is a mere $345,000 but the engine is a bit more robust: a 632-horsepower 12-cylinder gas guzzler. It also has just enough room for a driver and a passenger, plus those chips and ale.

You could put either car on a race track, although one engine will scream as it powers you from 0 to 60 mph in 13.3 seconds and the other will purr to the same speed in 3.4 seconds. Can you guess which one has the giddy-up? More importantly, both cars will get you through heavy traffic to the supermarket in exactly the same amount of time.

Okay, enough about cars. Back to laptops. For basic jobs like word processing, browsing the Internet, and playing solitaire, any current machine will do just fine, from a $600 bargain special to a $3,000 luxury model. If you're planning on doing a moderate amount of basic graphics or audio editing, or if you need to prepare and then deliver complex PowerPoint presentations, then you need a machine with a bit more horsepower (in the form of a faster processor and more memory). And if you've got to do some very demanding work and have special needs like an extra-large screen or some extraordinary multimedia assignments you may need to buy a Lamborghinia . . . I mean a top-of-the-line luxury model laptop equipped with above-the-ordinary graphics and audio capabilities.

No industry standards consistently divide laptop models into classes, so I've come up with some of my own. Feel free to modify them to meet your particular needs, update them as changes occur in the industry, and use them to make your own decisions on purchasing, upgrading, or holding on to your laptop.

The prices and configurations I am using are common in 2008. Throughout the history of personal computers, the trend has always been this: Prices go down and you get more and more for your money over time. But there will always be a price and performance difference between the latest and greatest, and the relatively oldest and least. Be careful out there.

## Basic laptop

This is the perfect machine to use as an extension of your desktop computer when you go out on the road or head off to class. It will process words, churn a spreadsheet, or communicate with the Internet just about as well as any other machine. In 2008, the low end of the market would have been considered near the top of the pyramid a few years ago. You could pay somewhere in the vicinity of $550 and receive the following:

- An Intel Celeron or equivalent CPU, running at about 1.8GHz in speed

- A set of capable but basic graphics chips built directly into the motherboard (*integrated,* as the techies like to say) and sharing the system memory (which means the total amount of RAM available to the CPU is reduced by the amount required by the graphics processor)

- A glossy, widescreen LCD of about 15.4 inches

- 1GB or so of RAM, shared with the graphics processor

- A combination CD-R and DVD player

- A large (but not huge) hard drive, perhaps about 80GB in capacity

- Basic I/O facilities including two or three USB ports, an ExpressCard slot, a built-in Ethernet port, and a built-in modem

- Built-in WiFi transceiver for wireless communication

- A 1.5"-thick box that weighs about 5.9 lbs

In less than two years since this book's first edition, the typical price for this basic machine has dropped about $100, the screen has grown over an inch, the hard disk drive has doubled, the standard memory has quadrupled, and WiFi has gone from optional to standard.

## Fully equipped road warrior

This is a model for travelers who need to do real work while they are away from their real desk, and it also has the facilities you need to create and display presentations on its own big screen or connect to a projector if you need to live really large. Expect to pay at least $1,500 and as much as $2,000 for something like this:

- An Intel Core 2 Duo processor or equivalent CPU with a pair of processors running at 2.0 to 2.6GHz

- A separate, high-end graphics card within the case with its own block of memory, adding more colors, higher resolution, and speed

- A separate audio sound card that delivers full sound production and capture facilities, well beyond the basic capabilities of built-in audio chips on the motherboard

- A high-resolution glossy widescreen LCD of about 15.4 inches, or for about $100 more, a 17-inch screen

- 3GB to 4GB of shared RAM, or dedicated memory for the exclusive use of the CPU

- A DVD read/write device that also works with CDs. The next great thing is a Blu-ray drive, which can also handle DVDs and CDs; prices are beginning to decline for the advanced drive but you can expect to pay a premium to go blue for a while.

- A larger, faster hard drive, perhaps about 200GB to 300GB in capacity, spinning at 7200 RPM

- A full complement of I/O facilities including as many as six USB ports, a FireWire port, S-video output, an infrared port, a PC Card slot, a built-in Ethernet port, and a built-in modem

- A built-in webcam mounted in the upper frame of the LCD, plus a microphone and speakers

✔ A fingerprint reader to add a highly personalized form of security to the login process

✔ A larger battery for extended usage

✔ A 1½"-thick box that weighs about 6 pounds

Since this book's first edition, the price of this highly capable road warrior has remained about the same, but has improved in many important ways. The CPU now has two processors and they're faster than ever; the installed RAM has gone up six- or eightfold; the hard disk has doubled or tripled in size; and bells and whistles include the webcam, the fingerprint reader, and a DVD burner. Oh, and the weight has dropped by a few pounds.

If you're determined to spend even more, you can pay as much as $3,000 for an "extreme" machine that comes with the latest and fastest CPU, the most capable graphics and audio subsytems, extra RAM, a larger hard drive, and other tweaks, bells, and whistles.

## Lightweight champ

For some users, you (or your laptop) can never be too light. And there's a lot to be said for such machines; just ask a chiropractor or physical therapist who's treated sore shoulders, stiff necks, and twisted knees from travelers. A few pounds can make a great deal of difference over the course of a week-long trip.

There has to be a tradeoff, of course, and it begins with a smaller screen and a lighter, slightly less capacious battery. Some users may also find the overall shrunken dimensions of a laptop are as small as they want to go; many lightweight models have reduced-size keyboards and pointing devices. Expect to pay about $1,500 to $2,000 for a little gem like this:

✔ An Intel Centrino Duo or equivalent CPU

✔ An integrated graphics chipset that shares the system memory

✔ A screen size of about 12 inches

✔ 1GB to 2GB of RAM

✔ A DVD read/write combination drive

✔ A mid-size hard drive, perhaps about 120GB to 200GB in capacity

✔ A good complement of I/O facilities including perhaps a pair of USB ports, a FireWire port, S-video output, an ExpressCard slot, a built-in Ethernet port, and a built-in WiFi transceiver

✔ A 1-inch box that weighs about 2.44 pounds

In 2008, Apple introduced a nifty little device called the MacBook Air, which shoehorns a 13.3-inch display, a keyboard, and a solid-state 64GB "drive" into a box less than ¾ inch thick and weighing short of 3 pounds. The price? Well, early buyers could expect to pay somewhere between $2,700 and $3,000, but some people can never be too rich or too thin.

# Entering the Box

I describe the laptop as a sealed box, and for the vast majority of people, that's the way it will always be. This is very different from a desktop PC, which is readily opened and is built with the expectation that it will be adapted, changed, or expanded.

The main reason the laptop box is sealed is that its internal parts are so tightly and intricately packed that it's not easy for an untrained amateur — no matter how experienced at fix-it projects — to reassemble it. The case is engineered to be tough but light, sealed against the elements but still able to exhaust heat. In addition to holding all of the pieces in a relatively secure box, it also is assigned the task of guarding against radio frequency radiation, which might interfere with other pieces of electronics. And finally, the parts within the case are mostly proprietary to a particular manufacturer — these aren't the same sort of components you can buy off the shelf at your nearby super-duper-computer center.

I won't ask you to pick up a screwdriver or a specialized tool to open the case of a laptop. That task is better left to a professional repair shop. Later on, though, I discuss those parts of the machine that are open to you, including memory slots and plug-in expansion bays. But just so you can say you do know what lies within, here are the major components inside the sealed box:

## Motherboard

A *motherboard* is the place that holds the principal electronics of the computer, with tiny etched wires (called *traces*) that connect attached components or sockets that hold removable chips. Branching off the motherboard are connectors to various types of memory, storage, and input/output.

In the original design for personal computers, what was called the mainboard started to be expanded through the use of smaller, attached boards of circuits and chips. The mainboard became the motherboard and the smaller collections of electronics the daughterboards.

Motherboards are very closely linked to the case that holds them; the mainboard from one maker's machine is unlikely to fit into the case sold by another, and only slightly less unlikely to move within the various models sold by the same manufacturer.

## CPU

The *central processing unit (CPU)*, or *microprocessor*, is the brain, or at least the manager, of all the data and instructions that pass back and forth within the machine. Most modern laptops use a modified version of the same microprocessor employed by desktop computers; designers have come up with many ways to reduce the amount of power that processors demand, which helps extend battery life and also reduces heat buildup (which also cuts down on power use by the fan).

Some of the most current microprocessors, including the Intel Centrino M, can adjust their speed and power use depending on the task they're performing. The Centrino technology includes a CPU, a supporting chipset, and a wireless transceiver. The chip itself is the Pentium M. If the computer includes all three parts, the manufacturer can call it a Centrino system; if it lacks the WiFi circuitry, then the laptop is called a Pentium M system.

Other Intel chips used in laptops include mobile versions of the Core 2 Duo processors, sometimes identified as Mobile Core 2 Duo, and the slightly less capable Core Duo processors.

Advanced Micro Devices, the only significant Intel competition in the laptop CPU marketplace, has its own series of highly capable microprocessors. Current chips include the Mobile AMD Sempron and the AMD Turion 64 X2 Dual-Core Mobile Technology.

## Memory (also known as RAM)

Memory is the place where the computer gets its work done. This is the scratchpad, the assembly place for your words, numbers, pictures, and sounds before you manipulate, display, print, or file them away in storage for future reference. Memory is more properly referred to as *random access memory (RAM)*, because the computer can reach directly into the chip to find a piece of information without having to go through everything else in front of it.

Another important thing to remember about RAM is that it's *volatile*, or temporary; it requires a near-continuous source of electrical power and regular refreshing of its contents. Let me put it another way: Turn off the laptop and RAM loses its memory.

And finally, more memory is generally better than less memory. Your processor works faster if it can work on data in RAM instead of having to retrieve it from storage (a hard disk, for example). The downside to more memory in a laptop is that the chips require power and also generate more heat, which fans must remove. Therefore, a battery's working time in a system with a lot of RAM is shorter than in a system with less memory.

## Chipset

If the CPU is the brain or the manager, then the chipset is the loyal, handpicked, and highly skilled support staff. The devices in the *chipset,* which must be carefully matched to the CPU by the laptop's designers, are in charge of executing the instructions put forth by the processor and determine the personality of the hardware side of the hardware/software equation. In almost every design, laptop processors and chipsets come from the same manufacturer; once again, the biggest maker of both is Intel.

## Input/Output

Where the motherboard stops, its *input/output (I/O)* ports and connectors begin. Modern laptops offer faster and more flexible means of communication than ever before, led by USB and WiFi.

# Foraging for Hardware

You buy into a tradeoff with the purchase of a laptop: It's unreasonable to plan on opening the box to make changes or add parts. Everything has to be done from the outside.

The good news, though, is that there is a huge selection of external enhancements. I will divide those improvements into two classes: plug-ins and attachments. Those two may sound like they're the same, and they're very similar. But here's the difference:

- *Plug-ins* slide into pockets, bays, and enclosed slots and travel with the laptop. In most cases they're locked into place with a latch or a screw. (They're still external to the innards of the case despite residing in their own plastic cocoon.)

- *Attachments* hook up to connectors, ports, or make electronic communion with wireless points of access including WiFi and infrared circuitry. Most must be disconnected and put in your carrying case or suitcase (or left behind) when you set out to travel.

## Plug-ins

Modern laptops typically come with one or more bays to allow easy interchange, replacement, or upgrade of certain components. They include the following:

- **Memory compartment:** Most machines come with a basic block of RAM and let you install one or more additional modules into connectors, which you access from the bottom of the case. (Most motherboard designs balance memory into an even number of *banks,* which is why a design with two or four slots is common.) These modules are usually industry-standard sizes and shapes; you don't ordinarily have to buy memory that bears the logo of the manufacturer of your laptop. Be sure, though, to exactly follow the required specifications.

✔ **Battery compartment:** Your laptop comes with a battery, and depending on your patterns of use, it may last for a year or two and sometimes longer before it fails or no longer holds a charge long enough to make it useful. You can purchase a replacement battery from your laptop manufacturer or a third party. Some users go to the trouble of buying and charging a second battery to take with them on long airline trips or for other situations where they might not be able to recharge the device or run the laptop from AC current.

✔ **Hard drive compartment:** Many laptop makers now attach their storage disks to quick-connect, quick-remove pockets or bays. This allows easy upgrading or replacement of a failed unit. As with other components, you may be able to obtain a replacement drive from sources other than the laptop manufacturer. Be sure to follow all instructions about removal and installation procedures; in almost every machine, you should never remove the hard drive while the laptop is powered up. The drive is usually locked in place with one or two small screws.

✔ **Optical drive compartment:** Some manufacturers make it easy for you to remove and replace the CD or DVD drive. You may be limited in your options for replacement here because of nonstandard carriers or connectors used by some makers, and you also must have the proper software driver to work with the machine. The drive is almost always held in place by several small screws.

✔ **WiFi module compartment:** You may find access to a small compartment that holds a matchbook-size circuit board that serves as a transmitter and receiver for wireless communication. Most manufacturers advise users against even opening the compartment because of regulations set by the FCC meant to limit spurious radio frequency emissions. Check instructions carefully before you consider removing or replacing this circuit board.

✔ **ExpressCard slot:** Most laptops can accept one or two credit-card-size enhancements here. The range of devices you can install here include WiFi transceivers for laptops that don't have built-in facilities, tiny hard drives, modems, Ethernet network interfaces, and many other devices. The older size and design for such plug-ins was called a PC Card; the newer and more flexible system is known as the ExpressCard.

## Attachments

The Swiss Army knife of the modern laptop is the USB port, and you may find one or as many as six ports. For many users the USB and the wired Ethernet or wireless ports are all you need to work with just about any external device or network.

Most — but not all — external devices require a separate power source and are generally used when the laptop is at a desk with an AC power supply.

In the list that follows, I've marked the ones that usually require independent power with an asterisk. You can attach these devices to a laptop:

- **Network:** If you need to upgrade an old machine or work around a failure, you can plug in the circuitry to exchange information with other computers or share devices, including a broadband modem for use of the Internet, or a printer attached to any other computer that's a member of the workgroup on the network. The common specification is called *Ethernet,* and it can use either a wired or a wireless (WiFi) connection to other devices.

- **Printer**\*: A printer can be directly connected to a laptop using the USB port. You shouldn't have to carry your own printer around with you; almost any USB printer can be attached and recognized by a current laptop running Windows. Older laptops and printers may want to communicate using a parallel port and connection; either the laptop or the printer can use a converter cable that changes parallel data to serial information (or the other way around).

- **Broadband modem**\*: You can directly connect to a high-speed cable or DSL modem to use the Internet. Most of these devices connect to a laptop through an Ethernet or USB port.

- **Scanner**\*: This useful device can import digital images of pictures or text; that information can be kept as graphics, or the text can be put through an *optical character recognition (OCR)* software program to convert it to editable data for use in a word processor. Scanners require a broad pipe to convey a great deal of information; most current models use (you guessed it, right?) a USB port. Some older scanners require a SCSI port, which isn't commonly offered on laptops, although once again some converters can stand between the scanner and the . . . USB port.

- **External hard drives**\*: You can easily add more storage with a plug-in drive; external drives can be as small and light as a videotape and attach to a USB or an eSATA port.

- **External optical drive**\*: Plugging in an attached CD reader or burner, or a DVD player or burner, is easier than installing a new one in your laptop. Once again: You'll make the connection through the USB or eSATA port.

- **Digital still or video camera:** Film? We don't use no film around here no more. Digital cameras have almost completely replaced film; in almost every situation, they're used in conjunction with a computer for storage, editing, printing, and transmission of the pictures. Almost all current cameras can output their files to a laptop using a cable to either the USB or the iLink/FireWire port.

✔ **Memory card reader:** An alternative to directly downloading using a cable from a digital camera is to use a card reader that plugs into a . . . say it with me . . . USB port on the laptop. Some readers are specific to a particular type of memory media, such as CompactFlash or SmartMedia, and some offer four to six slots intended to work with most of the common designs.

# Going Through Windows

It would be hard to find a computer user who hasn't been exposed to Windows — the operating system for PCs and PC-based laptops. (A small slice of the computer world uses Linux, which is the same idea, differently expressed; Apple users use that company's equivalent.)

But relatively few users understand the real purpose of the operating system and its interrelation with the hardware and software that sit (in logical terms) below and above it. Let me try to explain. The job of Windows is to

✔ **Manage the hardware.** Windows sits between the hardware and your applications with hooks into each. When a piece of software — a word processor, for example — wants to load a file into memory for editing, Windows receives the request and translates it into a command that the hardware can fulfill. Hardware must fit within certain specifications in order to work with PC motherboards and processors, but various components have differing capabilities; manufacturers develop a small piece of code called a *driver* that identifies hardware to the operating system.

✔ **Manage the software.** Similarly, software developers have a fairly wide latitude in the sort of tasks they can assign to their programs. However, there has to be a way for a single piece of software to interact uniformly with the nearly infinite combinations of hardware that exist within computers. The job of Windows is to adapt the software commands to what it knows about the capabilities of the hardware. Windows also allocates the use of the computer's memory and processor time so that various programs can coexist without conflicts and crashes. (Do I hear a guffaw out there? I'm with you . . . but it's true that with each successive release and update of Windows, the number of system crashes and other failures has gone down. May we all live to celebrate the extermination of the final bug.)

✔ **Manage the files.** If you have a hard time this morning remembering where you put your keys, consider the fact that a typical computer has to remember the location of tens or hundreds of thousands of programs, snippets of information, and complete files. (On my main work machine, my antivirus checking program most recently found something like 450,000 files worth checking . . . and half a dozen pieces of spyware it recommended for obliteration.) Windows oversees the creation and management

of a set of interlocked tables and indexes of files. It's all invisible to you,
but oh so important.

✔ **Show a pretty (and simpler) face.** For most users, this is what it's all
about: Putting lipstick on an electronic pig. Those of us old enough to have
used computers before the introduction of Windows (or Apple's Macintosh
operating system) remember that the screen was harsh and black. The
machine sat there stubbornly presenting nothing more than a command
prompt, a flashing dash that demanded that you, the user, tell it what to
do. It was your job to type in the proper command to launch a program,
format a disk, or copy or rename a file. The arrival of Windows put a *GUI*
(pronounced *gooey*) on the screen: a *graphical user interface.* A mouse or
other pointing device was presented and allowed to click here, pick up and
move something there, and even draw on the screen. Beneath that GUI,
Windows translates it all into commands to the hardware and software.

# Hitting the Internet

When laptops (and desktop computers before them) were developed, they were
thought of as independent islands. A *personal* computer was meant to be one
person's tool. But just as human beings are by nature social creatures, so too
have PCs evolved into interconnected members of a worldwide web of machines.
In fact, what once began as a sidelight — the interchange of electronic mail and
the ability to visit a collection of information at a "site" — has for many users
become the computer's main purpose.

Laptop users have especially benefited from this evolution. As you go out on the
road, you can now take your home or business office with you; you can exist in
*cyberspace* and no one has to know where you are when you send or receive files,
information, or mail. Think of what cell phones have done in an even shorter
period of time: If I'm not at my desk when someone calls my office, the call is
forwarded to my cell phone and I can answer almost anywhere in the world.

Laptop users can gain access to the Internet in several ways: by using a dial-up
modem in connection to the *plain old telephone system (POTS);* by WiFi interchange with a wireless point of access to a high-speed modem; or by connecting
(via wire or wirelessly) to an office or home network that includes a high-speed
cable or DSL modem.

Where exactly is this place called *cyberspace?* The best definition I know of is
based around a technology more than 125 years old: If you and I were to speak
on the telephone, our conversation doesn't take place where I am or where you
are. Our words, and the business we conduct, take place in a virtual world that
has no physical foundation: *cyberspace.* (The word itself was coined by novelist
William Gibson in his 1984 book, *Neuromancer,* and it referred to a vast network

of interconnected human and computer minds.) Today we call that place the *Internet,* and here's what it encompasses.

## The World Wide Web

The best-known part of the Internet isn't a thing, and it isn't owned or directly managed by any individual, company, or government agency. That's mostly a good thing, although sometimes a world without limits can be taken over by bandits, vandals, and other evildoers. The Internet is a *web* of interconnections between huge commercial, educational, and government systems and individual outposts like your personal laptop.

Becoming a citizen of cyberspace is as simple as obtaining access to the Internet. Bits and pieces of the web are managed by communication companies, *Internet service providers (ISPs),* and an international organization that oversees the issuance of *Internet protocol (IP)* addresses and domains.

I don't have time or space to name all of the things you can do on the Internet, but I list a few in a moment. I can confidently say, as a journalist who's been involved with personal computers since their birth more than a quarter-century ago, that almost none of these were even imagined back then: buying a car, selling a house, watching a movie, reading a book in a library 10,000 miles away, finding a recipe, consulting a doctor . . . get the idea?

## Electronic mail

For many people, electronic mail has all but replaced the neighborhood postal carrier for most of the essential letters. We receive bills, mash notes, credit-card statements, and even that most cherished of all postal items: junk mail.

E-mail is essentially a store-and-forward system. Here's what that means: You can send a message anytime and the recipient can pick it up whenever he is online. Messages travel from your computer to a server at an ISP or a web site, and is then routed from there to the server associated with the person you're addressing and on to its destination. The message moves at electronic speed, minus the generally insignificant time it takes to navigate through traffic jams at various routing sites. For that reason, physical distance makes little difference; when I send a message or a file by e-mail to a co-worker at her desk 10 feet away from me, my message (broken up into small packets that travel on their own and are reassembled at the recipient) takes a couple of dozen hops up and a couple of dozen hops down before it arrives.

(Just for giggles, I decided to use one of the many *trace* utilities you can find on the Internet to see the path from my office in Massachusetts to the location of the computer that holds www.hudsondreams.com, one of the web sites I own. The report showed that there were 30 different handoffs that began near my office, eventually going through New York City, Washington, D.C., Dallas, Kansas City, and eventually arriving in Wayne, Pennsylvania. Total time: 71ms, or just shy of a tenth of a second from here to there.)

### Instant messaging

If that's not quite fast enough for you, you can employ another technology that wasn't in the plans when personal computers were introduced. *Instant messages (IMs)* are intended for use in situations when both the sender and the recipient are at their computers and connected to the Internet; both parties make a connection to a central server, which routes messages between the computers at near-instant speed. The leaders include AOL Instant Messaging (AIM), Yahoo! Messenger, MSN Messenger, ICQ, and other services, including Google Talk and Jabber.

### Voice over Internet Protocol

And then you've come full circle, to the use of the computer and the Internet as a substitute for the telephone. You plug a phone or an entire housefull of phones into a special telephone adapter, which is connected to a broadband modem and through it to the Internet. The telephone adapter converts the analog rising and falling waves of a voice signal into digital packets that can travel over the Internet. Calls from computer to computer can be as cheap as free (although you do have to pay for Internet service); calls from regular phone to phone, using the Internet's facilities, are often included in the flat rate for *Voice over Internet Protocol (VoIP)* service.

# Organizing Files, Extensions, and Folders

One other important function of a computer — laptop, desktop, or mainframe — is as a place to keep your stuff. Although we're nowhere near the promised paradise of the paperless workplace, it's also true that computers are a great improvement over a filing cabinet (or in my case, piles of important papers on the desktop, stuffed into bookshelves, or arranged in dusty clumps on the floor).

For the convenience of humans (not the machine) Windows follows an electronic metaphor. Information of any sort, from word-processing documents to spreadsheets to graphic images, is stored as *files*. So too are programs, drivers, and settings.

Some files created by programs or the operating system have predetermined names; other files may be named by the program as they're created, and others, when you save a file that you've created, give you the chance to give it a meaningful name. (If you don't name it yourself, some programs apply generic titles like FILE001 or IMG001 or the like; just a little bit better are programs that attempt to name files based on the first line of text in the file, something that may or may not be meaningful to you.)

The operating system stores other information along with the name, including the date and time the file was last stored. Some other programs record additional information including the original date of the file's creation, the number of revisions, and other details. And many programs automatically create a backup version of an existing file when you open it for revisions; in case of catastrophe (or if you decide that changes you have made since the last time the file was saved are not worth keeping) you can open the backup file and save it under a new name.

There are no right or wrong names for files, except for two things:

- ✔ **Have a scheme that makes sense to you.** The more consistent and logical you are in choosing names, the easier it is to search and find files if you forget where you placed them on the hard disk.

- ✔ **Avoid using certain characters reserved for the computer.** You're somewhat protected here because the operating system will flat-out refuse to save a file that contains an "illegal" character. Just make sure to read the messages on the screen and don't assume that a file has been saved until you see the action performed.

Filenames under current versions of Windows can be as long as 255 characters and include any letter of the alphabet and any number, plus spaces, and special characters including $ % ` - _ @ ~ ! ( ) ^ # & + , ; = [ ].

That said, I recommend keeping filenames simple and relatively short. (By the way, the filename's maximum length includes the *path* to where the file is stored. If your files are deeply buried in a place like C:\windows\mydocuments\corey\dummies\laptops\quickreference\secondedition, you're starting in a hole 73 characters deep including the drive designation.)

The computer also does two things to help you find and work with files: assigns a filename extension that identifies a file as being of a certain type (a word-processing document, a music file, a photo or drawing, and so on) and because Windows is a GUI, it also gives files an icon. Some programs come equipped with their own icons, while others leave it up to Windows to find an appropriate or generic picture.

Filename extensions and icons serve two very important purposes: They make it easy to quickly identify files of a particular type, and they make it easy for the operating system to associate a file with the program needed to use it. Because of this feature, Windows allows you to double-click a filename and open it within the proper program.

The final component of managing your stuff is to use folders. Think of them as file folders, filing cabinets, or boxes on the floor: Their purpose is to help you organize your stuff. Windows tries to help out by offering a folder called My Documents, but that's only one level removed from just piling everything on the desktop.

# Part 2

# Built-in Stuff

A personal computer basically has just two dimensions: the front and the back. Laptops, which are at the same time both simpler and more complex than full-sized PCs, have fronts and backs of tops and bottoms, plus sides all around. The all-in-one-piece computer resides in the lower half of the clamshell. You'll find the components I'm about to describe on most modern laptops; your machine may differ slightly. In this part, I go into more detail on the built-in components of a laptop. Later on in the book I venture outside the box.

## In this part . . .

- Keeping your battery tuned up
- Using your sound system
- Storing data on disks, drives, and other media

# Checking Out the Screen

What do you see when you open up a laptop? On most machines, when you open the latch and move the screen to an upright position, what you see is a supporting frame around the LCD and a protective surface across the front of the screen to guard against damage and to deflect glare. If your laptop has Hollywood pretensions (or you're a laptop owner with Hollywood dreams) you may also have a tiny webcam built into the upper frame above the screen.

The very first electronic computers were essentially very large and very complex calculators. Remember those old sci-fi movies where the space cadet or the mad scientist would prance around in front of a console full of flashing lights? No screen, no printer: just light bulbs. Today's personal computers and laptops are very different; they're graphics-based devices. Although deep within its electronic chips the machine is still manipulating numbers, as a user you're working with pictures.

A screen is essentially an interactive television; you see a picture of a set of words, or a picture of an Internet web site that's based on the computer's conversion of numbers into an image. Going the other way, the computer is capable of interpreting the movement of an on-screen pointer to receive instructions from you. (Some special-purpose laptops have a touch screen that responds to finger taps or motions applied directly to the LCD. You've probably used this technology at a bank's ATM or an airline's automated check-in kiosk.)

The electronics for the LCD screen are enclosed within the upper part of the clamshell and they're relatively simple: a web of tiny wires that crisscross the screen at right angles to carry current that darkens or lightens specific spots (called *picture elements* or *pixels*), and on most machines a very small lamp that illuminates the screen background. The brain that determines which pixel should be light or dark is located in the lower part of the laptop.

There's not a whole bunch to say about the back (you might call it the *cover*) of the upper part of the laptop. Its purpose is to protect the LCD screen within, but don't mistake it for a bulletproof shield. Never place a heavy load on the cover — it's simply not that strong and you could end up cracking the screen or its wiring within.

Finally, hinges attach the upper part to the lower part and a flexible ribbon of wires connect the electronics of one to the other. These low-tech mechanical devices are a dangerous potential point of failure. Always use a gentle hand when you open or close the clamshell, and avoid hyperextending the screen too far back from an upright or slightly obtuse angle.

You can adjust the appearance of your LCD screen four ways. Two of the methods are physical adjustments, and two are electronic settings; it's up to you to find the best combination for your style of work and your tired eyes.

You can make a number of adjustments to the screen resolution, number of colors displayed, and other settings from within Windows — although I recommend that you take a very cautious approach here. The very nature of a laptop as an all-in-one box means that the computer, the graphics adapter, and the screen have all been matched by the designers and they're probably given the proper settings.

On a current machine using Windows Vista, you can get to the Display Settings dialog box in several ways. The most direct route is this:

1. Right-click any blank area of the desktop.

2. Choose Personalization from the pop-up menu.

3. Click Display Settings.

    Another pathway: Go in through the colorful Windows button at the lower-left corner of the taskbar. Choose Windows⇨Control Panel⇨ Personalization⇨Display Settings.

If your system uses Windows XP, the quickest way to the Display Properties dialog box (virtually identical to Display Settings) is to right-click any blank area of the desktop and choose Properties from the pop-up menu. (Or you can go in through the Start button at the lower-left corner of the screen, choosing Start⇨Control Panel⇨Display and clicking the Settings tab.)

However you get to the adjustment screen, here are your options on the Display Settings dialog box of Windows Vista or on the Settings tab of Display Properties available under Windows XP.

## Screen resolution

Windows will have automatically detected the built-in LCD and list it in the Display window. Resolution (Windows Vista) or Screen Resolution (Windows XP) reports how many picture elements *(pixels)* the adapter shoehorns across the width and height of the screen. On my widescreen laptop, the highest resolution is set at $1440 \times 900$ pixels and the system is optimized to work best at that setting. If you find you cannot work comfortably with the screen at that setting, you can reduce the resolution by moving the slider with the mouse. The lower the resolution, the less information is presented onscreen (and the quality of the image is generally degraded, but some people like or require it that way).

The choices presented here are the *native,* or recommended, settings for your particular monitor and graphic adapter combination; although you can use advanced tools to choose a different resolution, it's not a good idea. At best, nonstandard resolutions result in misshapen characters and images; at worst, they can damage the electronics.

## Color quality

This option (Colors in Windows Vista, Color Quality in Windows XP) specifies the number of available colors the system has in its palette. More is better than less, although the largest palette also requires more graphics memory and slows down the machine a bit. Most modern laptops give you a choice between Highest and Medium; they may have different names.

Highest color is sometimes called *32-bit* or *True Color.* They're all the same setting. Medium color is sometimes called *16-bit* or *High Color,* and again, the three terms are interchangeable.

You can experiment with the lower color setting to see if it makes a noticeable difference to your eyes.

If you burrow a bit deeper you may see advanced options that include a choice of refresh rate; you may or may not be able to make a change here, and you probably shouldn't risk damage to your screen or its electronics by doing so. I suggest you leave this technical setting at its default rate.

You may also find that your laptop manufacturer or the graphics chipset maker allows some advanced settings particular to your machine. These include adjusting the *aspect ratio* (the relationship of the width of the image to its height; on widescreen laptops some images or text may be stretched horizontally unless adjustments are made). In general, though, your laptop comes properly set up by the manufacturer and you should make changes here only *after* due consideration; make notes on any changes you might make so you can undo them if necessary.

On my most current laptop, right-clicking a blank space on the desktop offers access to Graphics Properties; this utility is produced by Intel to permit adjustments to the Graphics Media Accelerator on the motherboard. The utility isn't part of Windows and, confusingly, it duplicates some of the Display Settings options in Windows Vista.

## Screen brightness

This is an adjustment of the screen made from outside Windows; on most laptops a Function (Fn) key combination increases or decreases the brightness; some laptop makers also provide an onscreen adjustment panel for this. Feel free to try turning the illumination up or down until you see an image that's best for your eyes. You may find it necessary to adjust the screen in rooms that are overly bright or dimly lit.

Be aware that the brighter the setting, the more power the screen will draw. That isn't an issue if your machine is being powered through its AC adapter; if you're working off the battery, though, bright light means shorter working time between recharges.

Most modern laptops attempt to eke out the most battery life by automatically dimming the screen slightly anytime the machine isn't connected to an AC source. You can enable or disable this feature from the power mode software supplied by the manufacturer.

### Screen angle

This is the most direct manipulation of the computer possible: The angle at which you view the LCD affects the brightness and sharpness of the image you see. On most machines, the screen is designed to present the best image when the clamshell is open to a slightly obtuse angle, wider than a perfectly upright, 90-degree L.

Take care not to overextend the angle of the screen; that can put strain on the connectors between the upper and lower parts of the laptop. (And watch out for a too-wide angle anytime you use your laptop on an airplane's seatback tray table; if the screen is tilted too far back, it could be damaged if the passenger in front lowers the seat abruptly.)

## *Going with an External Monitor*

Attaching a second, external monitor to a laptop is as simple as plug, enable, and play. Nearly all laptops offer a VGA port essentially identical in specifications to the output of the same port on a desktop computer. Desktop and laptop external monitors have a few differences, though:

- ✔ Unlike on a desktop, a laptop system doesn't automatically send a video signal to the external video port. You have to turn it on with a keyboard command or (less commonly) with a software command.

- ✔ The external monitor requires its own source of electrical power, almost always from an AC outlet.

- ✔ Although you can use the VGA port from a laptop running on batteries, it drains electrical power and shortens the time you can work off the battery.

Relatively few laptops offer a DVI port to drive an LCD monitor with a digital signal. If that's essential to you, you may have to buy a converter that changes over the VGA port's signal. It won't be long, though, before digital outputs are common. See Figure 2-1.

Figure 2-1

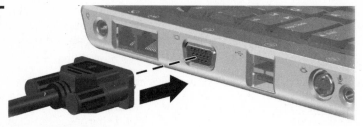

Courtesy of Hewlett-Packard Company

Why use an external monitor?

- ✔ To make a presentation on a large monitor or projection system. During speeches or presentations, I attach a high-resolution LCD projector to the VGA port to display my show on a theater screen.

- ✔ In a small presentation room, you might want one LCD screen facing you while you speak and a second monitor or screen facing the conferees watching raptly from around the table.

- ✔ To extend your output to a second screen. For example, as I write these words, my word processor occupies the LCD screen while I have a web browser running alongside. I can easily perform research and switch back and forth.

- ✔ To test or work around a failed LCD display.

## Configuring a second screen

Check the instruction manual for your laptop to find the keyboard command to enable the second monitor; you usually can choose to use the LCD only, the LCD and the external CRT, or just the CRT.

The next step is to instruct Windows how you want to use the second monitor. One screen is assigned as the primary monitor, home to the Logon dialog box when the laptop is first loaded and the default starting point for many software programs.

You're also permitted to select different screen resolutions and color quality settings for each screen, and can set a logical arrangement of the relation of one screen to the other — one above the other, or to one side or the other. (This isn't a minor issue; as you move the mouse off the edges of the primary screen, it arrives on the other screen based on this setting. The icon positions don't have to correspond with the actual position of one screen to another, but only the way in which items and pointers move and drag.)

## Setting screen positions

Here's how to identify and arrange the logical position of the built-in LCD and the external monitor. Begin by opening the Display Settings (Windows Vista) or the Settings tab of Display Properties (Windows XP) as outlined earlier in this chapter.

The dialog box in both Vista and XP includes an Identify Monitors button. Click it and a large 1 flashes on the primary monitor; a 2 flashes on the secondary display, if one is attached. See Figure 2-2.

**Figure 2-2**

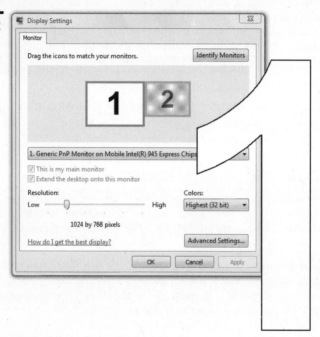

1. Click Identify Monitors (Windows Vista) or Identify (Windows XP) to display a large number on the built-in LCD and on the external monitor.

2. Click one or the other monitor icon and drag it to the position you like.

3. Click OK or Apply to view changes.

## Choosing the primary monitor

To choose or change the designation of one or another screen as the primary monitor, open the Display Settings (Windows Vista) or the Settings tab of Display Properties (Windows XP) as outlined earlier in this chapter. Then do this:

1. Click the numerical icon for the monitor you want designated as the primary monitor.

2. Click the open box to select Use This Device as the Primary Monitor to place a check mark or remove it; the check box is available only on the secondary monitor, not the one set as the primary.

### Extending a desktop across both monitors

When you choose this setting, you can drag items across your primary screen onto the secondary screen, or resize a window to stretch it across more than one monitor. Open the Display Settings (Windows Vista) or the Settings tab of Display Properties (Windows XP) as outlined earlier in this chapter. Then do this:

1. Click the numerical icon for the monitor you want to use in addition to your primary monitor.

2. Click the Extend My Windows Desktop onto This Monitor check box.

## Grabbing the Keyboard

Tapping the keyboard is the primary way to enter information into the computer. (Other input can come from selections made with the pointing device or mouse; from a microphone using speech-recognition software; and from forms automatically filled in by Windows.)

On machines sold and used in most of the world, the keyboard has all 26 characters of the English language. But it hardly stops there: The laptop in front of me is capable of directly recognizing at least 26 lowercase letters, 26 uppercase letters, 10 numerical characters, 32 symbols and punctuation marks, 10 function keys recognized by Windows or a program running under that operating system, and 15 commands such as Escape and Enter. Then there are 8 cursor and page-movement keys.

And finally, on my particular machine, 12 special Fn Shift-control keys issue commands to the hardware for things like adjusting the screen brightness or shifting output from the LCD to an external monitor. The same Fn shift can convert 15 characters to numerals for quick entry of large groups of numbers. The total: at least 154 direct keyboard inputs on this particular model. See Figure 2-3.

Full-size keyboards for desktop computers usually have a separate set of keycaps that are useful when you've got a long list of numbers to enter into a spreadsheet or database. A super-compact laptop keyboard has no room for a keypad. Instead, the right side of your keyboard can usually be converted into a numeric keypad.

F1 – F12 keys                    Numeric keypad

**Figure 2-3**

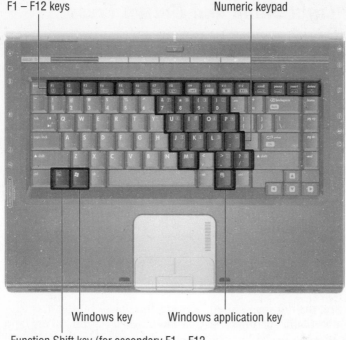

Windows key        Windows application key

Function Shift key (for secondary F1 – F12
functions and the numeric keypad)

Courtesy of Hewlett-Packard Company

**TIP** Laptop designers call this sort of embedded keyboard within a keyboard an
*overlay.* On most machines you see additional characters, numbers, or symbols
stenciled on the lower face of the Chiclets-shaped keys. The changeover
requires pressing the Num Lock key, which may be called just that or may use
some sort of obvious or less-than-obvious pictogram. Either way, press the key
combination once to turn on the keypad and press it a second time to return the
keyboard to its original key assignments.

On one of the machines I own, the magic switch is the Fn+F11 key combination.
On another machine, it is the Fn+F9 combination. Consult the instruction manual
for your laptop or experiment on your own to find out which Fn key to use.

You also find a Windows key on most laptops; this key displays the Windows
Start menu. And another key, called Windows Applications, displays a context-
sensitive set of menu choices for whatever lies below the onscreen pointer. (And
just for the heck of it, Microsoft added the Windows button to the Windows
Vista operating system; it appears — in its default position — on the screen in
the lower left of a laptop taskbar. The Windows button displays the same menu
as the Windows key.)

# Letting Your Light Shine and Button Press

Laptop manufacturers add all sorts of bells and whistles to their machines to try to differentiate one model from another. That's a good thing, assuming that the particular special features are ones you really need; at best you have buttons and lights you never use, but at worst the machine may be a confusing and crowded mishmash that gets in the way of productivity or fun.

These buttons and lights commonly appear on current machines.

## Turn on, turn off

On most laptops, the on/off button is on the top side; some models place it on the side of the case. Some manufacturers label the button as On, while others use a symbol, usually something more or less like Figure 2-4.

**Figure 2-4**

Depending on the designer's predilections, the power button may even have some color within it, surrounding it, or alongside it. On one of my laptops, the button glows a neon blue when the machine is powered up and running; the color changes to a mellow green when the computer is in standby or hibernation mode.

Again, depending on the design, you may be able to send your laptop into hibernation (or standby, or sleep) mode by tapping the power button. Or you may be able to initiate an orderly shutdown of your computer (closing applications and the operating system before removing power from the electronics) by pressing the power button.

## Multimedia controls

The current trend in all things portable and electronic is *convergence*. A cell phone becomes a music player that connects to the Internet and displays your pictures. A personal data assistant becomes a cell phone. A laptop becomes a CD player for music, a DVD player for movies, and connects to a WiFi system or a cell tower for Internet and telephone service.

Most current laptops now include a set of VCR-like pushbuttons to start, stop, pause, rewind, or fast-forward whatever media is currently active. When you're through crunching numbers in a spreadsheet, juggling sentences in a word processor, and sending e-mail to the home office, you can use your laptop to play a DVD movie or listen to music on CD.

## Indicator lights

Most laptops include at least one, and sometimes several, tiny indicator lights that give you information about your machine's status.

The hard disk drive indicator, which usually looks sort of like a stack of tiny dishes, is designed to flash or flutter when the drive's being read or written to by the computer. Why do you need to know this? It's one indicator that your computer is busy at work; if your screen isn't changing and you're wondering if the operating system has crashed (yes, it still does happen from time to time), you can look for a flashing hard-drive indicator.

Except in the case of dire emergency, you should never turn off your computer while it's busy . . . and a flashing hard-drive indicator tells you that it is.

Your laptop may also have a few other power-related indicators. On the very front of the edge of the keyboard platform on my bells-and-whistles laptop, I can see these lights:

✔ The first indicator, marked with a little electric cord symbol, means the computer is being powered by the AC adapter. (Did you guess that?)

✔ The second indicator, identified by the same symbol used for the power button (see Figure 2-4), means the power is on.

✔ The third indicator, marked with a symbol that looks kind of like an AA battery, of course indicates whether the battery is fully charged (on my machine, a happy green), in use (a cautionary amber), or near exhaustion (an urgent, flashing amber).

# Lighting Up with Batteries

At the heart of the laptop experience is the ability to take your machine with you almost anywhere you go; an AC outlet isn't necessary — at least for as long as the battery still has a charge.

Modern laptop batteries represent an incredible improvement in performance in the past decade. Today you can reasonably expect a lightweight battery about the size of a television remote control to power a laptop for three to seven hours, even as newer and more power-hungry components like high-speed processors, ultra-high resolution color LCDs, and DVD and Blu-ray players and recorders arrive.

The state of the art in batteries today is based on *lithium ion (LiOn)* technology. In addition to being able to hold a large charge in a small, relatively lightweight package, LiOn batteries are also relatively immune from the "memory effect" problem that afflicts other now less-common designs, including nickel cadmium

(NiCad) devices. *Memory effect* is a phenomenon that steadily reduces the battery's capacity if it's recharged without being completely discharged of its energy.

Be sure to consult your laptop's instruction manual for specific advice on how to get the most life from the battery.

## Hibernation and standby modes

*Hibernation mode* shuts down the laptop after it's saved the current state of the computer to the hard disk. This allows you to restart the computer a bit quicker than if it had been completely shut off; while the machine's hibernating, it doesn't draw power from the battery.

*Standby mode* puts the computer's current state into memory, which allows you to quickly restart the system without having to load the operating system and information from the hard disk. On the downside, the laptop requires a small amount of power from the battery to keep the information in memory, and if you run out of power while in standby mode, all information held in RAM is lost.

Your laptop's power mode software usually offers users several customization options. You may be able to instruct the system to automatically go into one or the other mode when the on/off button is depressed for a few seconds. Similarly, you may be able to go immediately into standby by merely closing the laptop cover.

Read the printed instruction manual or the installed electronic guide that's on most new laptops for details of your machine. You can also go to the Control Panel and select Power Options to see the options offered in that software; some laptop manufacturers may block the Windows power controls and direct you to use their own software.

Speaking for myself, I don't find hibernation all that useful; in fact, I find it sometimes presents problems with some of the utilities I use, including antivirus software, Internet pop-up blockers, and the like. I use standby if I know I won't use my laptop for 20 minutes or so, but I do so only after saving any data to the hard disk. The fact is that modern laptops come to life pretty quickly from a complete shutdown.

Nearly all current laptops also offer the opportunity to customize the demands on the battery depending on how you use your machine. Under both Windows Vista and Windows XP, you find an icon called Power Options on the Control Panel.

The range of controls offered to Windows XP users is generic, although many manufacturers added their own set of controls — such as the Power Management

Utility from Toshiba — to their machines. Windows Vista's Power Options utility is more comprehensive and has replaced most machine-specific software.

Either way, a power-management utility allows you to tell the machine whether to sleep, hibernate, or shut down when the power button is pressed or if the cover is closed while the machine is still running. You can also instruct the system to provide full brightness to the LCD when running on the battery, or to dim it slightly to save power.

Consult your machine's instruction manual and be sure to use the appropriate control program. In general, I set up my laptops so they run as brightly and fast as possible when running off the AC adapter and to sip as slowly as possible from the limited cup of power when running off the battery.

In a typical setup, like Figure 2-5, which is part of the Windows Vista suite of utilities, you can choose from among the following:

- ✔ Long Life or Power Saver: The most economical use of battery power at the tradeoff of speed and performance; see Figure 2-6

- ✔ Normal or Balanced: Gives reasonably high performance and brightness while conserving battery capacity

- ✔ High Power or High Performance: Delivers the brightest screen and the fastest CPU performance

**Figure 2-5**

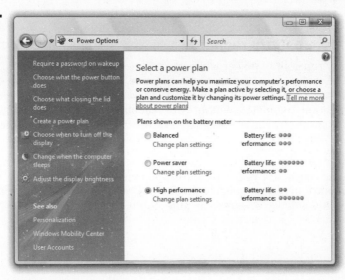

Some systems also offer special-purpose settings like DVD Playback. This option powers the screen and DVD player at full performance and turns off screensaver and auto shutdown utilities that might come on during a long movie.

**Figure 2-6**

## The ultimate battery recharge

If the battery runs out of power while you still need to use your laptop, and you're out of range of an AC outlet, one effective but low-tech solution can help: a second battery. You can purchase an additional laptop battery of the same design as the one that installs within your machine; it can charge when you're at your desk or in a hotel room, and you can store it in your traveling case as a backup. See Figure 2-7.

Another solution is to purchase an external battery pack that has its own recharger and plugs into your laptop to supplement the power supply as you travel. And you can buy an adapter that allows you run your laptop or recharge its battery from a power socket in an automobile.

**Figure 2-7**

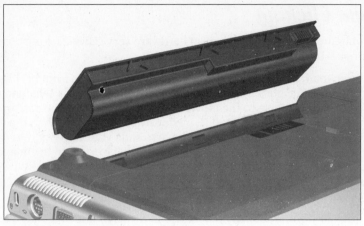

Courtesy of Hewlett-Packard Company

## *Listening to the Sounds and Furies*

Laptop designers have managed to squeeze an amazing amount of hardware into a small box, including the ability to generate a broad range of audio signals from a CD, a DVD, games, and the Internet. Most current laptops include a sound adapter that's similar to a basic sound card on a desktop machine.

So far, so good; you don't have a lot of room for a decent set of speakers or enough wattage to produce deep, vibrant sound and significant volume. However, if you purchase a widescreen laptop marketed as a multimedia device, it may have a bit of extra room. One of my more advanced laptops, a Toshiba Satellite P205, has room for larger speakers — a bit larger than a 25-cent piece — that bear the brand of Harman/Kardon, a well-known maker of home audio systems. I can't quite say that this particular laptop rivals the booming fidelity from the stereo system in my office, but the sound quality is markedly better than what I hear from more basic notebooks.

If you plug a good-quality headphone into the audio output jack of most any laptop, you'll be reasonably happy. And if you want to add to the bits and pieces of hardware you carry along with your laptop, purchase a set of external powered speakers that boost the music's volume and quality. These external speakers can run off batteries or an AC adapter.

# Pointing and Clicking

Two common types of built-in laptop hardware serve the same purpose as a separate, moveable mouse or trackball.

- **Touchpad:** A pressure-sensitive rectangle that sits in front of the spacebar, as shown in Figure 2-8. The onscreen insertion point or selection point moves in response to the movement of your finger on the pad: up, down, left, or right. The touchpad is, obviously, much smaller than the full LCD screen; this may mean that you have to slide your finger across the pad several times to get to the top or bottom, left or right of the image. (The laptop maker can offer some utilities and settings to speed up movement of the onscreen insertion point and in other ways more intelligently react to finger movements.)

- **Stick or pointer:** Usually embedded in the keyboard and extending slightly above the height of surrounding keys. Software interprets the push of your finger (and the amount of pressure applied) to move the cursor at varying rates of speed.

Touchpad

Touchpad scroll zone

**Figure 2-8**

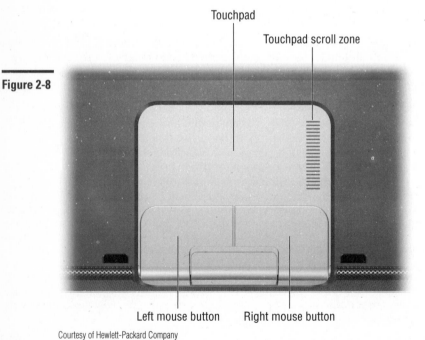

Left mouse button    Right mouse button

Courtesy of Hewlett-Packard Company

Under both designs — touchpad or stick — you also find a pair of action buttons nearby. The buttons are the equivalent of the left or right mouse buttons and are used to issue commands, make selections, or call up context-sensitive menus. Most touchpad designs also permit an alternate means of communicating the pressing of a mouse button; a double tap of the touchpad with the finger is interpreted as the same as a left mouse click.

Check out the Mouse Properties page, part of the Control Panel, to find out about available customization for the pointing device in your laptop. As an example, the touchpad's advanced feature settings in my most modern laptop let me assign specific tasks to the left or right buttons, as well as commands to taps made to any of the pad's four corners. A few laptop models add a scroll wheel between the two action buttons.

One important feature worth choosing — if it's not already part of the default settings for your laptop — is to enable snap-to functionality. When this feature's turned on, the pointer automatically appears in the default button of any dialog box you come to. This allows quick navigation through common tasks with a series of clicks or taps.

Other designs include a small *trackball* (an upside-down mouse that lets you move the cursor by rotating a ball), an *external mouse* (either full-size or a down-sized laptop version) that attaches to the USB or other port on the laptop, or a touch-sensitive or photoelectric *sensor screen* that reads finger movements and selections directly from the surface of a tablet or other specialized LCD.

Finally, you can add another form of pointing device by connecting it to the USB port or (on older machines) to a special mouse port (called a *PS/2 port*). If you do that, you may want to disable the built-in touchpad or stick; most laptops let you do that through a Fn key combination or in the Mouse Properties screen.

## Putting It in Storage

Modern laptops come equipped with a hard disk drive that holds files, programs, and settings that you create or load to from other sources. You also usually find one or another form of optical drive with removable storage media. Another form of removable storage coming into increasing use is *flash memory,* a form of RAM that doesn't need electrical power to retain information.

*Flash memory keys* have mostly replaced floppy disk drives on laptops. If it's absolutely essential that you read or write to a floppy disk, you can purchase a small external drive that connects to a USB port.

## Hard disks

A hard drive in a laptop is just like a hard drive in a desktop or tower computer *except* that it's much smaller, much lighter, and much less demanding of electrical power. It's also designed to be resistant to damage or problems caused by movement of the machine in which it resides, and the relatively robust case further protects it.

You have a reasonable right to assume that your laptop maker has selected a well-made hard drive; as a matter of fact, only half a dozen or so drive makers exist, and though one may be faster or hold more information than another, they're all pretty well made. A laptop manufacturer has no reason to install a drive that's likely to fail within the warranty period.

As a user, you should focus on two facts:

✔ Buying a hard drive that's too small for the sort of work you do is eventually going to cost you more. You have to do one of these two things:

- Replace the original hard drive with a larger one (and deal with all the related headaches of migrating your operating system, applications, and data from old to new).

- Add an external hard drive, which is an easy upgrade but requires more space in your laptop travel bag and will either eat battery power or require its own AC adapter.

✔ Although modern hard drives are very well made, and may last for many years (longer than you keep your laptop), this mechanical device quite possibly might suddenly stop spinning or otherwise refuse you access to the data stored on it.

You should always act as if today is the last day your hard disk drive will respond to your command. Know the three basic rules of storage safety:

✔ Back up your data.

✔ Update your backups.

✔ Back up your updates.

There are all sorts of automated backup systems, including tape drives and network storage. But most users need only to remember to store their essential data files in at least two places. In my system, when I am on the road, I burn a CD or make copies on a flash memory key every day. When I'm in my office, I make copies of live files from my laptop across an Ethernet to a hard drive in one of my desktop machines.

If you make backups every other day, the worst that can happen is losing a day or two's worth of work. With CD-Rs costing somewhere between ten cents and a quarter, they're the cheapest form of insurance you can get for your data (and for your money). Recordable DVDs are slightly more expensive, but hold much more data, while Blu-ray discs aren't yet a reasonable medium for casual backup use (although I'm sure prices will decline over time).

 Many hard disk drives die a silent death. One day they're working properly and the next they're as dead as an expensive doorknob. If you're lucky, you get some advance warning:

- ✔ Screeching or grinding sound from the drive

- ✔ Recurring garbling of part or all of a file

- ✔ An occasional hiccup where the drive won't come to life when you first apply power but comes back on a reboot

- ✔ An intermittent warning from the operating system or the BIOS that it can't communicate with the drive

- ✔ A specific alarm from a disk-monitoring software utility

- ✔ A steady (or irregular) increase in the number of bad blocks discovered by a system utility program

I'm always on the lookout for these signs, but I don't lose sleep over them — that is, unless I realize I've forgotten to make backups recently.

## Optical drives: CD and DVD

Most modern laptops come with a CD or DVD drive or a combination CD/DVD. And within that classification, you'll find CD-Rs and CD-RWs: devices that play CDs and record them on nonerasable discs (CD-Rs) or play CDs and record them on discs that can be written to and later erased and rewritten (CD-RWs). You'll also find equivalent read-only or read/write/erase DVDs.

The latest and greatest form of DVD is called Blu-ray, which is making its way into high-end laptop drives. The discs and the drives are, physically, nearly identical to DVD machines, but the media and internal laser are a different design. The difference lies in the vastly increased capacity of the discs, which can either store more data of the standard sort or produce ultra high-definition video.

The two biggest challenges facing laptop designers were shrinking the size and weight (and power demands, but that's a different issue) of hard drives and optical drives. Today's CDs and DVDs are mere shadows of the original size of these devices when they were introduced for PCs.

## Flash memory

How do you move a large amount of information from one non-networked computer to another? How do you safely store sensitive information separately from the laptop itself? One nifty little solution to these and a number of other data storage questions is the use of a small flash memory device (sometimes called a *memory key* or a *micro* or *mini drive*). These blocks of static, or nonvolatile, memory don't require a continuous source of electrical power to hold information; once you write to them, (in theory) they hold onto information indefinitely.

A flash memory device has no moving parts, and therefore can't be considered a true drive, but Windows treats it like one. Once you plug such a device into the system (through the USB port or hub), Windows assigns it a drive letter; it's read from or written to like a drive. The prices for these devices continue to decline even as capacities increase; as this book goes to press, the largest available memory keys could hold as much as 20GB, but you can be sure that even larger capacities are on their way.

Another version of nonvolatile memory is the tiny cards used in digital cameras, digital music players, PDAs, and some cell phones. Many modern laptops include a media slot that allows direct use of one or another of these devices. These cards, including Memory Stick, Secure Digital, SmartMedia, CompactFlash, and xD-Picture, can also be read from or written to like system drives.

## ExpressCard (also known as PC Card or Cardbus)

One way to expand a laptop's capabilities is to use a miniaturized device that fits into an ExpressCard slot. These devices, about the size of two or three stacked credit cards, plug directly into the laptop's system bus. An earlier, slightly larger, and less versatile version was called a PC Card or Cardbus (and way back when, a PCMCIA card); all three were different labels for the same thing.

For certain sorts of devices, an ExpressCard (or its ancestor) is a good way to semi-permanently upgrade your laptop; for example, you can use the slot to add WiFi to a wireless-less machine or a cellular modem for telecommunications. See Figure 2-9. Two card sizes are in use today:

 ✔ ExpressCard/54, which is the same width as a PC Card at 54mm or 2.125 inches although its depth is shorter and its connector is smaller

 ✔ ExpressCard/34, which isn't much bigger than a stick of gum at 34mm wide, about 1.3 inches

ExpressCards and PC Cards, just like USB devices, are *hot swappable;* this means that devices can be inserted or removed while the laptop's running, without concern about crashing the system or damaging the computer or card. (*Warm swapping* — removing a PC Card from a laptop that is in hibernation or standby mode — isn't allowed.)

Over time, most of these devices have been improved upon by faster and more capable external devices that attach to the laptop's USB port.

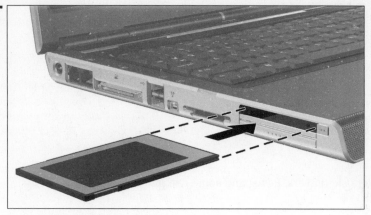

**Figure 2-9**

Courtesy of Hewlett-Packard Company

## Floppy disk drives

You may be asking, "What floppy disk drive?" Almost no new laptops give over space or resources to a floppy disk drive, ending a chain of compatibility that goes all the way back to the first personal computer. If you have an older laptop, you may find a drive (about the size and thickness of a deck of playing cards) on one side of your laptop; if you have an FD-less newer model and still need to use a floppy, you can buy a small, external unit that connects to a USB or special-purpose port.

# Ports

In its purest form, the laptop is an island unto itself, capable of performing nearly every essential task you could ask of it. Many people use it that way when they're betwixt and between home and office. But in its most powerful form, the laptop extends and expands itself by connecting to other computers and to a wide range of external devices. The magic doorways that make this possible are called ports. In this part you tour the ports on a modern laptop.

## In this part . . .

- Talking about communications technology
- Understanding networks

# *Communicating at High Speed*

When it comes to bringing in new information or sending out the fruits of your labors, faster is always better than slower. And modern laptops have made great use of new technologies to boost their ability to communicate. Today, a current laptop pays no price for its isolation from the comfort of the desktop.

## USB ports

The *Universal Serial Bus (USB)* may be one of the most accurately named pieces of technology in the entire history of personal computing, and that covers a whole lot of puffery and bafflegab. This system, introduced in 1996 with a slower version, has taken off like a rocket. Today an *almost* universal universe of devices and adapters can be plugged into a USB port.

Read the essentials you need to know about working with a USB port and devices:

✔ High-speed devices are designed to work with the newer and more capable USB 2.0 specification; nearly every current laptop offers a port of this specification, but some older machines may offer the older and slower USB 1.1 design.

A handful of machines shipped with the original USB 1.0 specification, and if you have one, upgrade. The easiest way to do this may be to plug a USB 2.0 converter into a PC Card or ExpressCard slot. You may need to disable the built-in and thoroughly outdated 1.0 circuitry through a selection on the BIOS setup screen.

✔ A USB 2.0 port can work with devices designed for that specification or for the 1.1 version; a slow device always operates at its lesser speed no matter how fast the port. Similarly, if your older laptop uses the slower port, the port limits the connection speed even if a faster device is attached.

✔ In addition to exchanging data in both directions, a USB device also receives electrical power from the laptop through the port. Therefore, if the laptop is run from its battery, anything plugged into the USB is also using up some of that stored electricity. That's little problem for most adapters and electronic devices. Some USB devices, including those with motors (such as external hard disks, CD, and DVD drives) may draw from the laptop's battery while others require their own AC power or a separate battery.

✔ A modern laptop may offer one or several USB ports but that's by no means a limit on the number of devices you can attach. Each USB port can be split into dozens of separate connection points through the use of a hub; for laptop users, other than the problem of clutter, the most significant problem is that the amount of power moving through the port is also divided up. (In theory, the limit is 127 devices per USB port.)

✔ USB cables have two different ends. The A end, which is flat and rectangular, plugs into the laptop or the hub output. The B end, which is more square (actually it has a square-like bottom and a three-sided flattop roof, sort of an angular D on its back), plugs into devices or as hub input. The connectors have a top and bottom and only insert fully when properly oriented.

Never force a cable into a port or hub.

✔ Some USB cables have an A connector at one end and a special-purpose connector at the other. Two examples are a cable that allows you to tap the stored energy in your laptop battery to charge a cell phone, and a cable (that converts the USB data stream to another format) and hardware (such as an old-style 25-pin serial connector).

✔ Certain devices, including flash memory keys and some WiFi adapters, plug directly into the USB port without a cable. Other devices connect the USB port for their own purposes and offer one or more extensions of the USB "chain" away from the laptop itself; these are sometimes called *pass-through* designs.

✔ Most USB devices are *hot pluggable,* meaning they can be connected to a laptop that's already running; the operating system recognizes the device and makes it available within a few seconds. (If it's the first time this device has been attached to the computer, though, you may have to install a software driver to help Windows work with it.) Many devices can also be unplugged from a running system without a problem; however, some older or special-purpose storage devices may require a special command (usually right-clicking a utility in the system tray — Windows XP calls it — or the notification area — as it is referred to in Windows Vista — at the bottom-right corner of the screen) to disconnect or dismount the attached equipment. See Figure 3-1.

**Figure 3-1**

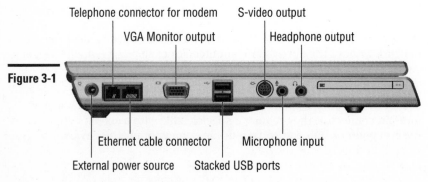

Telephone connector for modem

VGA Monitor output

S-video output

Headphone output

Ethernet cable connector

External power source

Stacked USB ports

Microphone input

Courtesy of Hewlett-Packard Company

### iLink/FireWire/IEEE 1394

This high-speed data specification is similar to USB 2.0 in many of its details. The IEEE 1394 specification was developed by an industry group for use with video recorders and other similar devices and called iLink; it was adopted by Apple (as FireWire) for its desktops and laptops.

The specification is supported by current versions of Windows, from Windows 98SE forward through XP and Vista. Whatever you call it, here are the important details:

- ✔ If your laptop doesn't have a FireWire port, you can add one or more by using an adapter . . . which connects to a USB 2.0 port or a PC Card slot. See Figure 3-2.

- ✔ The original specification (IEEE 1394) lets you connect as many as 63 devices to a single port, which is probably dozens more than you'd ever require; you can split each port by using an external hub. A newer specification not yet in wide use (IEEE 1394.1) permits more than 60,000 devices to connect to a single port, which is a mind-boggling number unlikely to be of value to most users, although it is a fun image to think of a room with 59,999 devices connected to each other and a laptop. Come to think of it, that sounds a bit like the testing lab in my office, which is a scary place.

- ✔ FireWire devices can be plugged into or removed from a laptop system that's turned on or off.

**Figure 3-2**

Courtesy of Hewlett-Packard Company

- ✔ One significant distinction of FireWire is that it can work as a *peer-to-peer* network without the need for a computer. For example, a FireWire video camera can directly exchange data with a FireWire hard disk drive.

- ✔ A FireWire cable usually has six wires, including two power conductors. Some devices, such as miniaturized digital camcorders, have a smaller four-pin connector; they require a special cable with a six-pin connector at the computer or hub end and a four-pin connector for the device.

### Infrared

You're almost certainly familiar with this sort of connection: The ubiquitous remote control channel changer for your TV or stereo uses focused pulses of infrared light (a color of red that humans can't see) to transmit information across a room. It allows information exchange for devices within line of sight of each other or that are in a position where the signal can be reflected its way; anyone who's ever bounced a TV control signal off the wall or ceiling should understand that sort of capability.

The advantages of infrared communication include its needs for relatively little electrical power and the unlikelihood that a casual interloper can intercept the information it carries outside the room where you're using it. The principal disadvantage: Its signal won't travel through walls or ceilings or over significant distances, and its communication rate is usually significantly slower than radio signals.

## WiFi

A wireless network is just like a wired network, except for the part about the wires. But the fact that wireless is missing a physical connection also opens up a whole new world for laptop users. Your laptop can fulfill its mission as a portable extension of your desktop, with the ability to tap into your e-mail, as well as the web, almost anywhere you travel.

Wireless communication (or *WiFi,* a meaningless label that is styled after the almost-forgotten home stereo nickname of HiFi, meaning high fidelity) uses a high-speed, short-distance radio signal. In technical terms, wireless computer communication commonly uses one or more technical specifications: 802.11a, 802.11b, or 802.11g. Newer designs are 802.11n and 802.11y, which have arrived in the market even though the industry hasn't agreed on all the specs. Any can carry an Ethernet network or make available a shared broadband modem connection to the Internet.

You need a few things to communicate wirelessly:

- ✔ A WiFi adapter, a combination of a radio transmitter/receiver, antenna, and circuitry to process outgoing and incoming signals for the laptop. Modern laptops include the entire shebang on a tiny card that fits into a pocket on the underside of the machine; the faster and more flexible -b, -g, and -n flavors of the 802.11 specification are preferable.

- ✔ An account with a wireless service provider or permission to use a private WiFi system. Actually, you may end up needing or wanting both. You can become a subscriber to commercial networks offering broadband WiFi in major cities as well as public areas at airports, hotels, restaurants, and bookstores for a daily, weekly, or monthly fee. And you will also find free access points at some coffee shops, restaurants, bars, and libraries.

   Most current laptops come with a utility to help configure and use the wireless communications facilities; you can also obtain generic controls from some of the companies that maintain hotspots. One example is the ConfigFree WiFi Utility from Toshiba. In Figure 3-3, my laptop is connected to the Internet by two channels — a 100-Mbps wired Ethernet cable and through a 54-Mbps 802.11g WiFi router.

**Figure 3-3**

## Bluetooth

This particular flavor of wireless interchange has been mostly aimed at ad hoc communication between handheld devices such as cell phones and PDAs. The idea works something like this: You meet someone at a trade show (or at a conference or at a singles bar) and electronically exchange all the information that you would place on a business card by pointing a pair of Palm Pilots or cell phones at each other.

On a laptop, a Bluetooth link is yet another way to easily exchange data with one of these devices. Not all that many laptops today offer this circuitry, instead preferring a WiFi transceiver; however, you can easily add Bluetooth to a laptop with an adapter that installs in an ExpressCard or PC Card slot or as an external device attached to a USB port. One of Bluetooth's strengths is that the hardware does all the work. After any two devices find each other, they negotiate with each other all the technical details of the conversation. We're beginning to see more Bluetooth in devices like hands-free headsets for cell phones and certain communications between laptops and PDAs (including Blackberry devices).

(The odd name Bluetooth, by the way, comes from Scandinavian history. Harald Bluetooth, king of Denmark in the tenth century, united Denmark and part of Norway. Scandinavia is a hotspot of cell phone and wireless communication and companies there chose the colorful name.)

# Enjoying Audio and Video

Although a laptop includes its own display device (the LCD screen) and sound system, many users need larger and more powerful ways to showcase their work and pump up the volume. For example, a road warrior giving a speech or making a presentation can write, edit, and generate a killer PowerPoint presentation on a laptop, but unless you're proposing to gather the audience to look over your shoulder at the LCD, you're going to need to output the image and sounds.

All current laptops include facilities to get multimedia out of your laptop. Some hardware is better than others; consider the options when you buy or upgrade your portable computer.

## VGA monitor connector

You can attach an external analog monitor or LCD, like those used with a desktop PC with a standard 15-pin cable. Most laptops require you to redirect the video signal from the LCD screen to the external monitor through a keyboard command. Over time, laptops will begin offering DVI ports that deliver direct digital communication to LCDs; if you have a standard VGA output, you must connect to an LCD that accepts an analog signal.

You should use this facility for a number of reasons:

✔ To output a video signal from the laptop to a video projector or large monitor to make a presentation

✔ When you're working at a desk with a larger monitor than the one built into your laptop

✔ To troubleshoot or work around a nonfunctioning built-in LCD screen

Many modern laptops also allow you to use both the internal and an external monitor at the same time. You can have the same image displayed on both, or you can send each one different pages of information; settings to assign multiple displays are made from within the Windows display properties screen.

Here's why you might want to use multiple screens:

✔ If you're standing at a podium and presenting via your laptop, you can have the projected image on your computer in front of you. This allows you to face your audience.

✔ If you're working at a desk, you can display different screens of information at the same time. For example, while I'm typing these words, I'm looking at a word-processor screen in front of my fingers, and at the same time I have an Internet browser open on a monitor off to the side. This allows me to do Web research (and check baseball scores) without closing or minimizing the word processor.

## S-video

This special-purpose connector, available on many higher-end laptops, transmits a high-quality video signal that can be used by better television sets and projectors. S-video (as in *separated video*) keeps the signal's brightness and color information on different wires, resulting in a sharper, brighter, and more colorful image. The alternative for TVs is a composite video signal, which squeezes all the image information onto a single wire. (Future laptops may offer *High-Definition Multimedia Interface [HDMI]:* connectors to output signals directly to a high-definition television. That would dovetail nicely with notebooks equipped with Blu-ray drives, allowing your portable computer to provide high-resolution audio and video to an HD television.)

The S-video connector on most laptops requires a matching four-pin male cable end; the connector has a positioning pin and a pair of notches to assure proper insertion. Examine the cable and connector before attempting to use them; never force a cable into place.

If you want to send an audio signal to the television or projector, you will have to run a second cable from the laptop. Some portable computers offer a round connector for use with an "RCA" cable; other laptops offer only a multipurpose headphone/external speaker output that uses a miniature plug. If you do not have a drawer full of every known cable in the computer, video, and audio world — like I do — you may want to make friends with a salesperson at a Radio Shack store.

## Microphone jack

*Jacks* are holdovers from the early days of electrical devices, a system to easily bring together open ends of a single wire, or perhaps two or three, in a temporary connection. Remember pictures of telephone operators connecting an incoming call to its intended recipient? The operator held a jack with two wires, separated by an insulator, and looked for the appropriate receptacle that could pick up the two signals. On computers, jacks and matching receptacles are used for simple circuits such as audio for speakers or input from microphones or amplifiers.

The input for an *unamplified* microphone is the simple sort of device you use with a small tape recorder. Most laptop computers offer a female connector that works with a ⅛" *monaural* (single channel) plug, although some may work with a *stereo* (dual-channel) plug.

Experts say the best type of microphone for a low-voltage circuit like the one on a laptop is generally an electric condenser design. If you connect a dynamic microphone, another common design, you may find that the sensitivity or volume level is lower than you prefer.

Consult your instruction manual for any unusual specifications for your laptop. You may find some laptop makers specifying the use of a 3.5mm plug; in most cases that metric size, though not identical, is close enough to work with a ⅛" plug.

If your laptop permits use with a stereo plug, consult the manual to see how it handles a mismatch. For example, one model of HP Pavilion laptops with a stereo port advises that if a monaural microphone is used, it will record the same information on both channels of any file you create. Another model, this one with a monaural port, advises that if a stereo microphone is plugged in, the laptop will record the output of the left channel only.

## Line-in jack

Some high-end laptops aimed at use in multimedia assignments (such as editing soundtracks) may have a *line-in jack,* which accepts an amplified audio signal. An example of this sort of signal would be the output of a stereo system, a portable audio device, or a tape recorder.

Consult the instruction manual for your laptop, and if necessary, an electronics retailer for advice on adapting your audio equipment or laptop for special recording purposes.

If your laptop isn't equipped with a line-in jack, you can purchase an external sound adapter that connects to the USB port. One example: Creative Technology's USB Sound Blaster.

## Headphone jack

The miniature socket here (on most laptops designed to mate with a ⅛" or 3.5mm plug) outputs an audio signal you can use with personal headphones.

The best sound quality comes with headphones with an impedance of 24–32 ohms; *impedance* is a measurement of a form of resistance to the flow of electricity. What this means to you is this: Use a lightweight, low-impedance headset like those specifically designed for use with portable music systems rather than one of those heavyweight professional-style headsets you may have for your home stereo system. You'll get better sound, higher volume, and longer battery life.

The same signal can also be directed to a set of external amplified speakers or accepted by some external stereo systems or television sets; these external devices need to amplify the signal by using their own electronics and power supply.

On most systems, plugging a headphone or other type of audio cable into the socket automatically disables the laptop's tiny internal speakers. To protect your hearing, always adjust the volume level before placing headphones on your ears.

## Line-out jack

This socket delivers a lower-level signal that can be directly used by external devices with their own amplifiers, such as tape recorders, VCRs, and stereo systems. You'll find line-out circuitry on certain high-end multimedia laptops.

Consult the instruction manual for your laptop, and if necessary, an electronics retailer for advice on adapting your audio equipment or your laptop for special recording purposes. You can add line-in and line-out capabilities to a laptop through an external sound adapter that connects to the USB port.

# *Networking for Fun and Profit*

Networks serve two very important purposes: They connect one computer to another for information exchange, and they allow network members to share hardware, including storage devices, printers, and modems (including those that connect to the Internet).

The first generation of laptops had to be adapted to offer a wired interface to a network. The second generation came with a built-in *network interface card (NIC)*. And today's current machines build on that wired connection with a high-speed WiFi wireless transmitter/receiver.

## Ethernet

Most modern laptops offer built-in network interface circuitry and a port that allows direct wired connection to an Ethernet system. You need a cable with an *RJ-45 plug* (an oversized cousin of a familiar telephone connector) and a hub, switch, or router that provides access to the network.

It's also possible to directly connect the Ethernet port on a laptop to the equivalent port on a desktop with a single cable and set up a peer-to-peer network between the two. You can purchase Ethernet cables (called *CAT-5* in some descriptions) of almost any length, although you'll have more reliable communication and you or your laptop are less likely to suffer a tumble if you keep the cables short and neatly coiled.

Network use requires no additional hardware; the software side of "enabling" a network is accomplished by Windows settings. If you have an older laptop that doesn't offer a built-in network interface, you can add one by using an adapter that inserts into an available ExpressCard or PC Card slot or that attaches to a USB port.

## Telephone modem

In the early days of personal computers, dial-up networking to the Internet or direct connection to another machine was a marvel; today for most users dial-up has been mostly relegated to a backup to much faster and easier-to-use wireless or broadband services. However, you may still find it useful to use a standard telephone line to call an *Internet service provider (ISP)* when you're on the road and end up in one of the few remaining places where no wired or wireless broadband networks are available.

Most modern laptops include a built-in modem and connector. (You may hear mention of something called a *soft modem,* which is a design that uses some of the computer's microprocessor and memory to emulate a hardware modem; a soft modem is perfectly acceptable for most users, although it may slow down other tasks that run at the same time.)

To use a modem, you need a standard telephone cable with an RJ-11 connector and an outlet in the home, office, or hotel room that has an analog dial tone.

An analog signal is the most common phone system in homes, but laptop users should take extra care before plugging into a hotel or office system that might use a higher-voltage digital system; in the worst of mismatches you could fry your laptop's circuitry or at least damage or destroy the internal modem. Ask before plugging into an unknown system.

If you must use a digital phone system with your laptop's built-in analog modem, purchase an external digital-to-analog converter. One end of the converter plugs into the wall and the other end offers a safe outlet for the laptop.

# Pairing Up with Legacy Ports

Sometimes the Old School is your only choice; there may not be a good reason to throw away a perfectly good printer or scanner just because it was designed in the ancient era that existed before USB, FireWire, and other technologies.

## Parallel/serial ports

Few modern laptops still offer these *legacy* connectors; both have been supplanted by the more flexible and much faster USB system. Still, if you have an older printer or scanner, you may need to communicate with it using a *parallel cable* (a collection of eight wires to carry each of the individual bits of a computer word, plus additional wires for status, power, and other purposes). A dwindling number of older devices expects to receive an old-style serial cable with nine wires.

You can easily add a parallel or serial port, or both, with a converter that plugs into a (you guessed this, right?) USB port. One such device is offered by Keyspan; that company's Port Replicator provides one serial and one parallel port and replaces the one USB port with two more.

## Keyboard/mouse ports

Many older laptops offered a circular keyboard, a mouse port, or both, for use with external devices. The design uses a small connector with a notch and location pin to assure proper installation; most current desktop computers still use this design.

Today, though, this special-purpose port has been mostly replaced by the USB port and by keyboards and pointing devices that directly plug into that port. You can, though, purchase a converter cable that plugs into a USB port at one end and gives you a PS/2 keyboard and mouse port at the other.

# Windows Essentials

Leaving aside its computational abilities, Windows is, at its heart, an organizational device. It provides essential services to software, organizes file contents and locations, and instructs the hardware to print, transmit, receive, sing, or dance. In this part, you look at the essential places of Windows; I concentrate on the newest version Windows Vista without overlooking the still very widely used previous edition Windows XP.

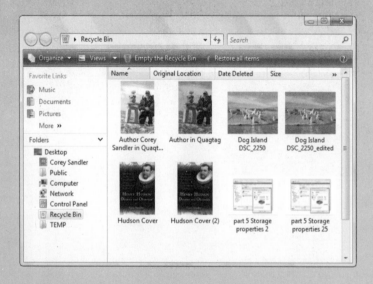

## In this part . . .

- ✔ Accessing the Control Panel, My Computer, My Documents, and My Network Places
- ✔ Trashing the Recycle Bin
- ✔ Using the Start button, taskbar, and system tray

# Accessing the Desktop

The *desktop* is home base for Windows, the starting and ending place for your sessions. It's also the place where you keep your most essential doorways to what lies beneath. The Windows Vista desktop looks very much like that of Windows XP, except Vista users can add a new group of interactive *gadgets* on a Sidebar. In Figure 4-1 you can see some examples of gadgets on my system.

**Figure 4-1**

Although the desktop is presented as a sort of Windows symbol, that doesn't mean that you can't make major changes to its appearance. Windows Vista users can change the background image (called *wallpaper*) and otherwise personalize this way:

1. Right-click a blank part of the desktop.

2. Choose Personalize.

3. Click one of the available options.

   Those options include Desktop Background, Windows Color and Appearance, and Theme. To change the Display Settings, click the menu item with that name.

Change or remove the background image under Windows XP with these steps:

1. Right-click a blank part of the desktop.

2. Choose Properties from the pop-up menu. See Figure 4-2.

**Figure 4-2**

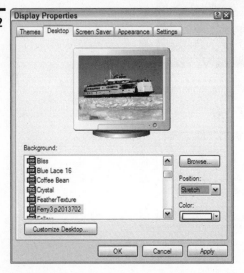

Windows XP users can also change the *resolution* (the size of pixels displayed on the screen) and the number of colors in the display palette by choosing the Settings tab from Display Properties. You can do the same from within Windows Vista by choosing Personalize⇨Display Settings. See Figure 4-3.

Laptops generally have a less flexible assortment of resolutions (and other advanced settings, including refresh rate). If the manufacturer properly configured the laptop (a reasonable assumption if you've purchased a device sold under a recognizable brand name), you aren't offered settings that the component can't give.

Make notes on the *default settings* (as delivered by the manufacturer) before changing anything; this allows you to restore them if you decide that your adjustments aren't improvements. Use your written copy of settings as backup to the automated System Restore utility available to users of Windows Vista or XP.

**Figure 4-3**

# *Biting into the All Programs Menu*

One way to find or start a program is to display the All Programs menu from Windows. (Three other ways: Double-click a shortcut displayed on the desktop; click a shortcut in the taskbar; double-click the name or icon of a file associated with a particular program.)

Under Windows Vista or Windows XP (in the Classic mode), you can get to All Programs by clicking the Start button (on the screen) or the Windows key (on the keyboard) and then choosing All Programs. See Figure 4-4.

Choose a program from the ones listed in the menu. Major programs have their own line and icon listed; some of the lesser programs and utilities may be listed on submenus that lie beneath category names like Accessories or Games. The most minor of programs may not be automatically granted a place here at all; you need to find its icon on the desktop or taskbar or execute a command from the Windows Run line. To instruct Windows to load and run a program from All Programs, click a program name.

Figure 4-4

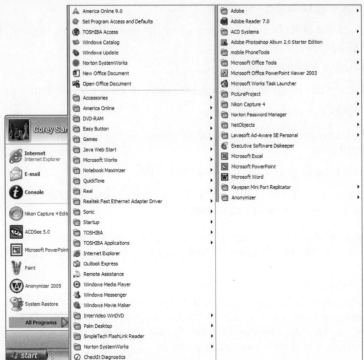

## The Startup submenu

Any programs you place in the Startup submenu are automatically loaded and run when Windows is first started. Some applications will insist on putting themselves into Startup as part of the installation process; this may or may not fit with your preferences. A program that unnecessarily loads with Windows will use up some of your available memory and slow the operating system and its applications.

To stop a program from automatically starting, move it from the Startup submenu to another submenu. Do this by clicking and dragging the program name to another submenu. If the icon is a shortcut to launch a program, you can delete the icon without removing the program itself.

## Creating a desktop shortcut to a program

For quick access to a program you use often, consider creating a shortcut on the desktop. Some programs offer to do this for you at installation.

Here's one way to make a shortcut:

1. Click the Start button (onscreen) or the press Windows key (on the keyboard).

2. Choose All Programs.

3. Locate the program for which you want to create a shortcut.

4. Right-click the program name.

   Left-clicking would launch the program, which you don't want to do right now.

5. From the pop-up menu, choose Send To⇨Desktop.

6. Press the Esc key on the keyboard, or click outside of the Start menu to close the submenus and menus.

The resulting shortcut on your Desktop can be moved anywhere on the screen for your convenience. To launch the program from the shortcut, double-click it.

### Organizing the All Programs menu

You can change the order of icons on the All Programs menu: Click and drag the icon you want to move. You can also rename most folder names and delete shortcuts or entire folders by highlighting an entry on the Start menu and then right-clicking. Choose Delete or Rename.

# *Boarding the Control Panel*

You can adjust much of your system's personality and functioning through the Control Panel. When Windows was first installed on your computer, it took note of hardware within the case and added some control features. As software and hardware were later installed, the panel was modified to offer more settings.

You can display the Control Panel (shown in Figure 4-5) several ways:

✔ Click the Start button (onscreen) and choose Control Panel from the menu.

✔ Press the Windows button (on current keyboards) and select Control Panel from the menu.

✔ From any Windows Explorer window (including My Computer, My Documents, My Music, My Pictures, and My Network Places), click the down arrow on the address bar, and select Control Panel.

Under Windows Vista or XP you can choose from two display and operational modes: Classic and Category. Classic view shows all the icons in one window (with icons or by name or purpose), while Category does a bit of organizing to place them within groups of similar subject matter. (Classic is for people who prefer to read names of programs and utilities; Category [shown in its Vista version in Figure 4-6] is for people who like their items pre-sorted into categories and grouped under pictures. The same programs are available under either scheme.)

**Figure 4-5**

**Figure 4-6**

# Coming to My Computer (Also Known As Computer)

You have to wonder if some Microsoft designer was thinking about computer newbies when this important Windows component was given its name. My Computer (under Windows XP) and Computer (Windows Vista) are the literal labels for a screen that displays icons or names for all internal and currently attached external hard disk drives, devices with removable storage such as CD or DVD drives, and the topmost folders for your documents, including My Documents, My Music, and My Pictures (for XP systems) and the slightly less familiar Documents, Music, and Pictures on Vista-based machines. If you have any scanners, digital cameras, or other external input devices attached to your computer and powered up, they may also be listed here.

You can display the My Computer (or Computer) window several ways:

 ✓ Double-click the Computer or My Computer icon on the desktop if your system has one there or if you have placed a shortcut there. See Figure 4-7.

 ✓ From any Windows Explorer window in Windows XP (including My Computer, My Documents, My Music, My Pictures, and My Network Places), click the down arrow on the address bar and select My Computer. (The Windows Vista equivalents: Computer, Documents, Music, Pictures, and Network.)

 ✓ Click the Start button (onscreen) or the Windows key (on the keyboard) and choose My Computer or Computer.

**Figure 4-7**

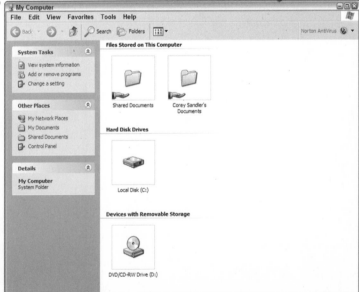

My Computer or Computer is a good starting place when you want to work your way through the folders on various disk drives in search of a file or a program.

You can also find information about attached disk drives from this screen. Right-click the icon for a drive and choose the Properties command. The Properties screen includes such important details as the drive's total capacity, as well as the space in use and the space available. You can also initiate one of the built-in disk drive utilities: error checking, defragmentation, and backup by clicking the Tools tab. (If you've installed a third-party hard drive utilities program, you'll probably prefer to use that program's utilities instead. The non-Microsoft software company may add its own tab to the Properties window as part of installation. If not, you'll have to launch the utility program separately.)

# Dealing with My Documents (Also Known As Documents)

Another literally named window, My Documents (XP) or Documents (Vista) is the default folder for your documents and files. Many software programs automatically offer to store files within this folder or a subfolder of this window. See Figure 4-8.

You're not required to store your files under this umbrella, although it's a good idea for most users. The key to creating additional subfolders in this window is to differentiate by name between the horror novel you're writing and the terrors of your banking statement.

**Figure 4-8**

You can display My Documents or Documents several ways:

- ✔ Double-click the My Documents or Documents icon on the desktop if your system has one there or if you have placed a shortcut there.

- ✔ From within any Windows Explorer window, click the down arrow on the address bar and select My Documents (XP) or Documents (Vista).

- ✔ Click the Start button (onscreen) or the Windows key (on the keyboard) and choose My Documents or Documents.

To create a subfolder, follow these steps:

1. Right-click a blank area of the My Documents or Documents window.

2. Select New⇨Folder.

The resulting subfolder is given the even more literal name of New Folder, which doesn't go very far toward helping you organize documents; before you store documents within the folder, rename it something more meaningful.

In most installations, Windows automatically creates subfolders called My Music and My Pictures (or Music, and Pictures) for use with, you know, music and pictures. Again, you're not required to use these locations for particular files, but most users probably should accept this organizational scheme.

If you've set up your Windows installation to allow individual users to have their own identity (and require them to log in and sign on with a unique user name and password), then each user will have a separate My Documents or Documents folder, but won't have access to the files in another user's folder. The only exception: systems set up to give someone *administrator rights.* On your personal laptop that might be you; if your employer owns and controls your machine, the information technology or computer services department may reserve those rights for themselves.

# *Entering the Network and Sharing Center*

The Network and Sharing Center is one of the hearty utilities added to Windows Vista. The Center brings together many basic and advanced settings, including the rules for discovering available network devices and sharing attached resources. See Figure 4-9.

You can turn each element on or off, and clicking the down arrow alongside each one explains its purpose and implications for each user. As with many of the improvements brought by Vista, this tool is valuable not so much because it brings new features but because it gathers features that have been inserted into earlier versions of Windows and displays them in one place with a set of logical categories.

**Figure 4-9**

# Finding Out about My Network Places (Also Known As Network)

If your laptop is part of a *local area network (LAN),* whether connected by wire, radio signal, or infrared, Windows is set up to track connected locations in My Network Places. (Have you figured out by now that My Network Places is the name under Windows XP, and Network is the moniker bestowed by Windows Vista?) See Figure 4-10.

As you set up a network and choose to *share* resources on other machines or on certain network-available devices (printers or detached storage), their names appear here. You can also add a location on the Internet, usually a *file transfer protocol (FTP)* site used by some organizations as a form of external storage.

You can click folders displayed in My Network Places or Network to perform various actions on files held on other computers: You can copy, move, rename, or delete files just as if they resided on your own laptop.

**Figure
4-10**

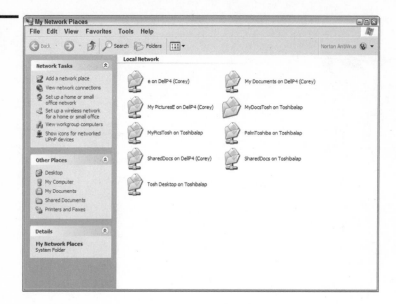

## Displaying Network Places

You can display My Network Places or Network, or access the same information held within those window, several ways:

- ✔ Double-click the My Network Places or Network icon on the desktop if your system has one there or if you have placed a shortcut there.

- ✔ From within any Windows Explorer window, click the down arrow on the address bar and select My Network Places or Network.

- ✔ From within the File Open window of most applications running under Windows, click the down arrow on the address bar and select My Network Places or Network. This imports the same list of locations present in the network window into the File Open window, allowing access to the files. You can also place files in a network location by using the Save or Save As command from within an application, and clicking the down arrow on the address bar to select My Network Places or Network.

- ✔ Click the Start button (onscreen) or the Windows key (on the keyboard) and choose My Network Places or Network.

## Removing the Network icon from the desktop

My Network Places or Network may appear on the desktop even if your laptop isn't part of a LAN; it depends on how your laptop maker configured the standard installation of Windows. There's no harm in leaving it there, but here's the drill if you want to remove it. For Windows Vista users, follow these steps:

 *1.* Right-click an empty space on the Desktop and choose Personalize.

    Or, go to the Control Panel and click the Personalization icon.

 *2.* From the tasks in the menu pane (on the left side of the window), click Change Desktop Icons.

 *3.* Click Network to remove the check mark.

    While you're in the neighborhood, you can also remove other icons from your desktop, including Computer, User's Files, Control Panel, or Recycle Bin.

 *4.* Click OK twice.

 *5.* Close the Control Panel.

For Windows XP users, follow these steps:

 *1.* Go to the Control Panel and click the Display icon.

 *2.* In the Display Properties dialog box, click the Desktop tab.

 *3.* Click the Customize Desktop button to display the Desktop Items dialog box.

 *4.* Click My Network Places to remove the check mark.

    While you're in the neighborhood, you can also remove other icons from your desktop, including My Documents, My Computer, and Internet Explorer.

 *5.* Click OK twice.

 *6.* Close the Control Panel.

# Foraging Through the Recycle Bin

The Recycle Bin is an environmentally friendly waste receptacle for your files that can save your bacon if you react within a timely manner after an accident or a change of mind.

When you "delete" a file from any version of Windows (or from within software that runs under Windows), the file isn't actually scrubbed from the hard disk surface. Instead, its name changes so isn't listed in ordinary indexes. It stays there until the system needs the space; then the file's removed from the drive and the space it occupied is available for storing new information, which is written over the former file.

In between the "deletion" and the overwriting, Windows offers the Recycle Bin, which fills up from the bottom with discarded files. Once the bin is full, the oldest files are released to the system to be written over. Before that happens, though, you can go to the Recycle Bin and instruct the system to *recover* (in XP lingo) or *restore* (offered in Vista) individual files or a whole group of files. See Figure 4-11.

**Figure 4-11**

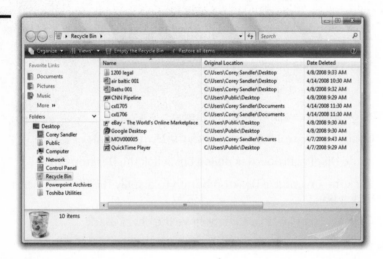

To open the Recycle Bin, right-click its icon on the desktop and choose Open or double-click the icon. You can organize and work within the Bin several ways:

- ✔ List the deleted files by name, deletion date, modification date, size, type, or other criteria. To adjust the listing order, choose View, Arrange Icons By, and then select the scheme you prefer.

- ✔ Restore all deleted items by clicking Restore All Items. Restore individual items by clicking them and then choosing Restore This Item. If you hold down the left mouse button you can click multiple individual files to select them for a group restore.

- ✔ Clean up. Delete individual files by clicking them and pressing the Delete key on the keyboard; dump all files by choosing Empty the Recycle Bin. When you delete a deleted file in this way, you end the ability to restore a file from this utility. (However, some third-party utility programs allow careful users to search their hard disk drives for files they've deleted but aren't fully overwritten with new material.)

Note also that if you install a utilities package such as Norton SystemWorks, that program modifies and expands the Recycle Bin to add features. Its basic function and appearance remain similar to the Microsoft Windows original. You'll also find automated recovery systems for files, such as the Unerase Wizard, which is part of Norton Utilities from Symantec. See Figure 4-12.

**Figure 4-12**

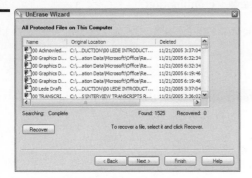

# Getting Going with the Start Button

So many instructions, settings, and commands and so little space on the screen — that's the problem presented to Windows users who have anything more than one or two basic programs on their laptop. The solution is to make use of the Start button's very flexible expanding facilities (or to the taskbar and system tray or notification area, which display open programs as well as a set of quick-launch shortcuts). This section explores each of these power tools for Windows users and shows you how to customize them to meet your style and preferences.

## Start button

The Start button is the place to go to start most programs, control panels, and Windows actions. Confusingly, it's also the place to go to *stop* Windows and shut down the computer.

The Start button is usually at the left corner of the taskbar, which is usually located at the bottom of the screen. However, you can move the taskbar to the left, right, or top of the screen, and the Start button travels with it.

When you click the Start button, it displays the Start menu. You can display the Start menu several ways:

- By clicking the Start button on the taskbar
- By pressing the Windows key found on most modern keyboards
- By pressing the Ctrl+Esc key combination

To close the Start menu, click outside of it or press the Esc or Windows key on the keyboard.

## Start menu

A list of quick program shortcuts appears on the left side of the Start menu. See Figure 4-13.

**Figure 4-13**

The top half of this section holds assigned shortcuts; usual residents include your Internet browser, your e-mail client, and the Control Panel. The shortcuts are considered *pinned* in place; you can "unpin" an icon by right-clicking it and choosing that option. You can delete an icon the same way. To add an icon to the pinned area, click and drag its icon from elsewhere on the Start menu. The bottom half of this section automatically stores recently used programs to make it easier to get to them.

At the bottom-left corner of the Start menu is the key to opening a list of nearly all the programs and utilities installed on your laptop: the All Programs button. On the right side of the Start menu is access to top-level folders including My Documents, My Recent Documents (automatically kept current by Windows), My Computer, My Network Places, and more on a Windows XP system, or the Windows Vista equivalents Documents, Recent Items, Computer, Network, and others. You also find one-click shortcuts to the Control Panel, Help, Search, and Run commands.

## Changing the Start menu style

With the introduction of Windows XP, the Start menu received a sleek makeover with more information and cascading submenus. But if you prefer to stay with a simpler, less flashy, retro look — Microsoft politely calls it the Classic style — you can change the design:

1. Right-click the Start button and choose Properties.

2. Choose Taskbar and Start Menu Properties.

3. Click Classic Start for a menu that looks much like the version used in Windows 98SE. See Figure 4-14.

4. Click OK to make changes.

**Figure 4-14**

## Adding or removing Start menu items

As with much of the Windows look and feel, you can customize some of the Start menu elements. To do so from the Windows XP menu, and not the retro Classic view, follow these steps:

1. Right-click the Start button and choose Properties.

2. Click the Customize button to display the Customize Start Menu dialog box, shown in Figure 4-15.

3. Make your settings.

   The General tab lets you specify icon size, the number of recently used programs displayed, and whether your browser and e-mail client are in the pinned section. Note also the Clear List button; it wipes clean the slate of recently used programs. Some users don't want others to see where they've been working lately.

4. Click the Advanced tab to make more changes to the Start menu.

5. Click OK to make changes.

**Figure 4-15**

# *Honing in on the System Tray (Also Known As Notification Area)*

The *system tray* (Windows XP) or *notification area* (Windows Vista) is home to utility programs that generally load with Windows; although you can usually start or stop these programs by left- or right-clicking the small icons that live here, on most systems the tray serves as a notification area. For example, on my machine I can look at the icons in the system tray to see if my antivirus program is on guard and my intelligent *uninterruptible power supply (UPS)* is fully charged.

Depending on the software, if you start a utility after Windows has loaded, it may temporarily take up residence in the tray as well. As an example, if you load AOL Instant Messenger, the program shows an icon to indicate that it's running in the background.

Double-clicking usually brings up a control panel for the programs appearing here. In most cases you can right-click the icon for actions that include opening, exiting, and switching profiles for these programs. You can add or remove items as you like from the system tray, but you cannot totally remove the tray from the taskbar. Some programs, despite manual removal, are particularly insistent on occupying a space here, reinstalling themselves the next time your laptop starts. The only solution for some of these programs is to completely remove them from the system.

## Adjusting the icon display

You can instruct Windows to show all the icons in the system tray all the time, hide all icons, or just show those that are currently active. See Figure 4-16.

**Figure 4-16**

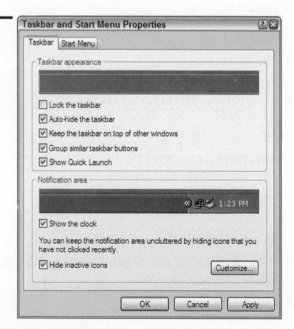

The most common setting prevents inactive icons. To make that setting, do this:

1. Right-click a blank area of the system tray or the clock.

2. Choose Properties from the pop-up menu to display the Taskbar and Start Menu Properties dialog box.

3. Click the empty box alongside the item called Hide Inactive Icons. Placing a check mark in the box enables that instruction; removing the check mark disables it.

You can also individually control the behavior of most icons (but not all — some manufacturers write their utilities in a way that force full-time display of the icons for their programs) by setting individual instructions. Here's how:

1. Right-click a blank area of the system tray or the clock.

2. Choose Customize Notifications. See Figure 4-17.

   This command may be unavailable if you haven't enabled Hide Inactive Icons as noted earlier in this section. You will see a list of programs that have been assigned a place on the system tray.

3. Click any name in the list; the instruction on the Behavior column changes to a drop-down menu with the following options:

   • Hide When Inactive

   • Always Show

   • Always Hide

4. Select a behavior and repeat for each icon you want to control.

5. When you're finished, click the OK button.

## Displaying a clock

For many users, the system tray serves as worthwhile home to a small clock. Here's how to turn the time display on or off:

1. Right-click a blank area of the system tray or the clock.

2. Choose Properties from the pop-up menu.

   The Taskbar and Start Menu Properties dialog box appears.

3. Select the Show the Clock checkbox to enable it. Deselect to disable it.

4. Click OK to exit.

**Figure
4-17**

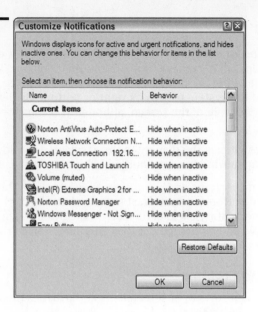

**Displaying the volume control**

The volume icon offers quick access to the software side of the audio controls in your laptop. (A rotary dial or slide switch may also reduce the volume. Most users want the software levels at their maximum setting for speakers, allowing speaker volume adjustment with the dial or switch.)

Follow these steps to instruct Windows whether to display the volume control:

1. Open the Control Panel.

2. Click the Sounds and Audio Devices icon.

3. Select the Volume tab if it's not already displayed.

4. Select Place Volume Icon in the Taskbar to display volume control. Deselect to disable it.

   While you're in the neighborhood, familiarize yourself with the Mute option. If this box is checked, nothing you do on the software or hardware side is going to convince your laptop to play sounds through its speakers.

5. Click OK to close the dialog box.

# *Leaning on the Taskbar*

The taskbar displays buttons for each program currently running or for each open window on the desktop, but it can also house additional toolbars. The strip is usually in the middle of the information strip of Windows with the Start button to its left or top, and the system tray to its right or bottom. By default, the taskbar is located at the bottom of the screen, although you can move it to the sides or top.

Clicking one of the buttons switches the display to the associated window and makes it active. Any other open windows are shuffled behind the active window.

You can also install program shortcuts on the taskbar; they appear in the Quick Launch section between the buttons and the Start button on the left or bottom end of the taskbar. Add a shortcut by clicking its icon on the desktop and dragging it to the taskbar; remove one by dragging it the other direction or right-clicking and selecting Delete from the pop-up menu.

## Adding toolbars to the taskbar

If you're the sort who enjoys all sorts of onscreen bells and whistles (and clutter) you can add toolbars to the taskbar:

1. Right-click a blank area of the system tray or on the clock to display the pop-up menu.

2. Choose Toolbars.

3. Click the toolbar name to add or remove it from the taskbar.

The available toolbars follow:

- **Quick Launch:** This collection of shortcut icons, which allows you to quickly load programs, may be the most valuable toolbar. You can add individual program icons by dragging them from the desktop or another window; remove them by dragging or by right-clicking them and selecting Delete. (Icons you drag into place are copied; the original icon remains in place on the desktop or other window.)

- **Address:** This toolbar offers direct access to a web site or a program on your computer; all you need to do is type in an address or program name and then click Go.

- **My Computer:** One- or two-click quick access to the same information found on the My Computer window.

Some programs offer their own toolbar to install here as well.

Toolbars can be *carefully* moved with the taskbar. To do so, the taskbar has to be unlocked (more about this later). To move a displayed Toolbar, move the mouse pointer to its left edge (if it's on the bottom or top of the screen) where you find a dimpled area with little dots. Click and drag the toolbar within the taskbar.

Note that toolbars don't always follow Microsoft's precise rules and may not cooperate when you try to move them, or may act unexpectedly.

## Moving the taskbar

You can move the taskbar from its standard position at the bottom of the screen to the top or either side. (Note that most instructions in manuals, books, and online documentation assume that the taskbar is located at the bottom.) Here's how to make a move:

1.  Point the mouse to a blank part of the taskbar.

2.  Click and drag to one of the edges of the screen. The taskbar snaps into a position when it's in an allowable location.

3.  Release the mouse button to place the taskbar.

## Locking the taskbar

Some users find that they're prone to accidentally moving the taskbar as part of other actions they may take on the desktop. And some users who share their machines with others (without a separate log-in) may want to keep the other person from repositioning the taskbar. The solution is to lock the taskbar:

1.  Right-click a blank area of the system tray or the clock.

2.  Choose Properties from the pop-up menu (Windows XP only).

3.  Click Lock the Taskbar.

4.  Click OK.

Locking the taskbar also prevents toolbars within it from shifting and hides the lip that serves as a handle for moving it.

## Resizing the taskbar

You can make the taskbar deeper or wider (to allow more buttons) or reduced (to take up as little space as possible). You can't resize if it's been locked.

To resize, do this:

1.  Point the mouse to the outside edge of the taskbar.

    If the taskbar is at the bottom of the screen, the outside edge is its top; if it is along the right side, the outside edge is its left side, and so on.

2. When the pointer is a two-ended vertical arrow, click and hold the left mouse button and

   • Move the pointer up or down to expand or contract a taskbar on the top or bottom of the screen.

   • Move the pointer left or right to expand or contract a taskbar on the left or right side of the screen.

3. Release the mouse button.

### Hiding the taskbar

I'm a minimalist; I prefer the taskbar be unseen unless I need to use it. Other users, more used to TV news shows that have six or eight different moving and blinking tickers and indicators, may want all of their options spelled out right before them.

You can choose to have the taskbar shown at all times, or have it *Auto-hide* to see it only when you bring the mouse pointer into its hiding place. To activate or deactivate Auto-hide, follow these steps:

1. Right-click a blank area of the system tray or on the clock.

2. From the pop-up menu, choose Properties to display the Taskbar and Start Menu Properties dialog box.

3. Click the Auto-hide the Taskbar check box to disable or enable the function.

4. Click OK.

# Sidling Up to the Sidebar

Any well-traveled person will tell you that you never can have too many gadgets. On the hardware side, my kit includes a flash memory key to transfer data to and from other laptops, a set of converter plugs and cables of every type I can lay my hands on, a small screwdriver, and a roll of duct tape. On the software side, I carry a DVD with a backup copy of the operating system and an emergency recovery disc from a troubleshooting utility program.

With the advent of Windows Vista, Microsoft introduced a set of electronic gadgets that are in a third class: customizable, miniature programs that allow you to use your laptop as a window on the world. (Most depend on a wired or wireless connection to the Internet.) For the record, this idea was borrowed from a similar concept, introduced by Apple, called widgets.

Windows Vista comes equipped with a basic set of gadgets that allow you to do things like monitor the weather almost anywhere in the world, follow stock market ups and downs, watch a mini news ticker, or browse through images. Gadgets also arrive as an assortment of clocks, calendars, contacts, and to-do lists.

On my machine I keep an eye on the Dow Jones Industrials (just to upset me), the local temperature and weather, the meteorological report from the next place I expect to visit, and other essential information like, say, the exchange rate between the U.S. dollar and the Norwegian krone.

By right-clicking within a blank area of the Sidebar and selecting Add Gadgets, you can open up the display of supplied gadgets. You can click a button to get more gadgets from Microsoft's Live Gallery web site, which contains verified utilities. (You can visit it at http://gallery.live.com.)

You can also add Gadgets by clicking the plus sign in the small black bar at the top of the Sidebar, shown in Figure 4-18.

And you will find other gadgets offered by commercial or amateur authors on the web, although I recommend exercising caution in loading any program — especially one that is in near-constant connection to the Internet — from a source that could possibly be compromised by malware authors.

**Figure 4-18**

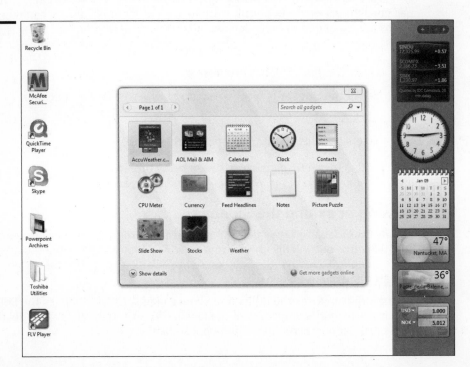

## Moving and configuring the Sidebar

The standard position for the Sidebar is (you guessed it) on the side — the right edge to be precise. You can drag it over to the left edge. And you can even change the metaphor by detaching gadgets from the sidebar and allowing them to float anywhere on the desktop.

Windows determines the Sidebar width. Depending on your laptop LCD's width and aspect ratio, it usually spreads about an inch off the right or left border of the screen.

Gadgets with a + indicate that they can be expanded with a *fly-out* that provides additional information or customization. For example, a stock ticker may fly out with more details of averages or specific trades.

The key to adjusting gadget appearance and operation is the Sidebar Properties window; you can get to it by clicking the Start button and typing Sidebar Properties into the search panel on the Start menu. Another way to the same window: Click the Sidebar Properties icon in the Control Panel.

If you want to keep an eye on the various gadgets in your Sidebar while you're working on other things — that is, of course, the purpose of Windows — you can have it permanently occupy one side of your screen even when other programs are maximized. This works especially well on a widescreen LCD, which has enough real estate to permit working with other applications; running programs are expanded to the Sidebar's outside vertical border.

To keep Sidebar on top, follow these steps:

*1.* Open Windows Sidebar Properties.

*2.* Select the Sidebar Is Always on Top of Other Windows checkbox.

*3.* Click Apply.

   To change this setting, remove the checkmark.

You can also toggle the Sidebar between being topmost or lower down by pressing the combination of the Windows key and the spacebar.

## Closing or exiting the Sidebar

*Closing* the Sidebar is equivalent to minimizing a program; the various gadgets are still active but will disappear from view. Right-click the Sidebar and choose Close Sidebar. To reopen the Sidebar, right-click its icon in the taskbar notification area and choose Open.

*Exiting* Sidebar closes the utility and all its gadgets. It also removes the Sidebar icon from the notification area of the taskbar. To exit, right-click the Sidebar icon in the taskbar notification area and choose Exit.

# *Storage*

Take a look at how you can control and manage the devices that hold your files: text, music, pictures, programs, and settings.

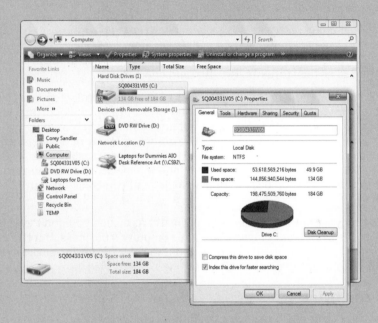

## In this part . . .

- ✔ Comparing binary math
- ✔ Using a CD or DVD
- ✔ Bringing back deleted information

# A Quick Understanding of Computer Math

This is a *Quick Reference* and I promise to be brief and simple, but it's important that you have a grasp of at least the basics of computer math. You need to know the difference between a bit and a byte, a megabyte and a gigabyte, and just enough binary math to know that it's not the same as decimal logic.

Why bother to understand how a computer counts? Because you live in a world that mixes mathematical metaphors.

Humans get along pretty well in a system derived (and supported) by the fact that most of us have ten fingers; we discover at an early age that as we progress from right to left, each digit is based on 10 times the value of the previous digit. Think of 123 as this: three 1s, two 10s, and one 100.

For a computer, though, thinking in leaps of tens is generally too complex for its tiny brain. Instead, nearly every computer ever developed works on a much simpler *binary* system. Each value in a computer number can have only two values: 0 or 1, or yes or no, or true or false. So, a computer's way of dealing with that same number would be this: 01111011. Here's how to translate that, again from right to left: one 1, one 2, zero 4s, one 8, one 16, one 32, one 64, and zero 128s. Do the math (switching back to human logic) and you come up with 123 in decimal math.

That's it — your entire course in binary math. As a user, you don't ever have to use this sort of binary logic; that's the computer's business. But the mixing and matching begins when you think about the size of storage devices (and memory) for a laptop computer.

## Bits and bytes

The smallest unit of measure in a computer is the *bit,* which is just a single 0 or 1 in a string of information in an 8- or 16-bit computer *word.* Back to my example: 01111011 (in digital translation, 123). That word could represent a particular color in an image file, a specific tone in an audio file, or a character code from the keyboard. (From the keyboard, 01111011 transmits the curly bracket — { — to be displayed on-screen or stored in a file.)

The next step up is a *byte,* which is made up of eight bits. Everything your computer does, and everything it stores, is constructed of strings of bytes; think of a byte as a character in a word. Older computers manipulated words made up of 8 bits or 1 byte, while most modern machines are based around 16-bit (2-byte) or 32-bit (4-byte) words.

"Aha," you may be saying, "my computer has 512 *megabytes* of RAM, and so that means it has the capacity to hold 512 million bytes." That's correct . . . sort of. When computer designers began thinking beyond 0s and 1s to much larger numbers, they adopted mostly Greek prefixes for bytes: kilo, mega, giga, and tera for (roughly) one thousand, one million, one billion, or one trillion. But in a binary world, these values were based on powers of 10: $2^{10}$ is 1,024, which is slightly larger than 1,000. As numbers go up, that error becomes larger and larger.

Here are the common abbreviations in computer math, their real value, and their incorrect but commonly used digital values.

| Name | Abbreviation | Digital shorthand | Real value |
|------|-------------|-------------------|-----------|
| Byte | B | 1 | 1 |
| Kilobyte | KB | 1 thousand | 1,024 |
| Megabyte | MB | 1 million | 1,048,576 |
| Gigabyte | GB | 1 billion | 1,073,741,824 |
| Terabyte | TB | 1 trillion | 1,099,511,627,776 |

And so the bottom line: Your laptop's 200GB drive has the capacity to store something like 214,748,364,800 characters of information, which is in the neighborhood of 215 billion. In actuality, that number's reduced by 20 to 30 percent because the computer needs to devote some of the space for things like indexes and markers, as well as separators, between the bytes.

And one more thing: Hard drive manufacturers (and the laptop makers who sell their devices) have an unpleasant habit of mixing and matching binary and digital math when it's to their benefit. For example, a drive may have the capacity for something like 19.5 billion characters in digital math; the maker (or its marketing department) may call that a 20GB drive.

Between the laboratory and the store shelf, the real capacity of that drive has lost 500 million characters because of rounding up to an even number, plus an additional 184 million or so characters because a number that started as a digital value is being expressed as a binary one.

What this means to you is this: Be sure you're comparing binary to binary or digital to digital when you appraise the size of a drive.

## Alphabet soup

Disk drives are assigned letters of the alphabet; they can also, additionally, be given a name.

Harkening back to the original PC, A is reserved for a floppy disk drive. If your laptop has such a device, that is its drive letter; if none is installed, the system skips over A to begin with C.

Which raises the question, What happened to B? Once again, this is a holdover to assure compatibility with some very old machines that someone, somewhere may still be using. On the very first PCs, before hard disks were common, there were often two floppy disk drives; B is reserved for a second floppy.

The first hard disk drive is almost always assigned C. Many programs and Windows itself are designed to install themselves on that drive. Letters D and up, all the way to Z, are assigned to later hard drives and then to removable CD or DVD drives and other such devices.

# Driving a CD or DVD

CDs were developed to hold music and they first arrived in computers as a kind of large-capacity floppy drive; software makers jumped aboard to use their capacity of 600 to 800MB as a means to deliver their programs. Similarly, DVD drives were first envisioned as a way to deliver full-length video to home entertainment systems. But they quickly made the move to players that could hold as much as 4.7GB of information for the use of computers.

In the next section I describe the latest and greatest form of optical disk drives now available for laptops: Blu-ray systems.

Today, that sort of read-only function is still available on laptops for loading software or data, or for playing audio or video on the road. But engineers have gone well beyond that, creating new classes of CD and DVD *writers,* which can burn a disc in desktop and laptop machines, and CD and DVD *rewriters,* which can write a disc with information and then go back and erase or write over that information (much like a hard disk drive).

Discs for the two systems are nearly identical in physical dimensions but use different designs. CD drives can only work with CDs; most modern DVD drives are capable of reading CDs as well as DVDs and writing and rewriting to certain types of DVDs.

Just to make things difficult, there were at one time no fewer than five competing sets of specifications for DVD, and they weren't all compatible with each other. If your laptop is only capable of reading a DVD, it should work with any commercially produced disc, but you have to experiment to see whether it can successfully play back the contents of recordable DVD produced on a computer.

You can check the details of your installed optical drive and make some settings by going to your device's Properties screen. See Figure 5-1. The following are among the ways to get to that screen:

✔ Control Panel⇨System icon⇨Hardware tab⇨Device Manager; then double-click DVD/CDRW drives to display a Properties screen.

✔ Open My Computer. Right-click the CD/DVD device shown under Devices with Removable Storage. From the generic DVD/CD-RW Drive Properties screen, choose the Hardware tab and then right-click the drive you want to examine; select Properties.

**Figure 5-1**

One more thing: DVDs are limited by international regions intended to protect against copyright transgressions. If you buy a movie in the United States, the licensor of that piece of intellectual property may not have the right to sell the film in Brazil, for example. This won't make a lot of difference to most people, but just in case, you should be aware of your machine's region setting. See Figure 5-2.

Read the instructions carefully; laptops generally permit only a limited number of changes to the setting before they're made permanent. (The only way to get around this is to replace the hard drive, or perform a low-level format to wipe it clean before reinstalling Windows.)

**Figure 5-2**

MATSHITA UJDA760 DVD/CDRW Properties

General | Properties | DVD Region | Volumes | Driver | Details

Most DVDs are encoded for play in specific regions. To play a regionalized DVD on your computer, you must set your DVD drive to play discs from that region by selecting a geographic area from the following list.

CAUTION  You can change the region a limited number of times. After Changes remaining reaches zero, you cannot change the region even if you reinstall Windows or move your DVD drive to a different computer.

Changes remaining: 4

To change the current region, select a geographic area, and then click OK.

Afghanistan
Albania
Algeria
American Samoa
Andorra
Angola
Anguilla

Current Region:  Region 1

New Region:

OK    Cancel

| DVD Flavor | What It Does |
|---|---|
| DVD-R or DVD-ROM | Basic specification for commercial DVDs; discs produced for this format can be played on nearly all modern laptop players as well on home video DVD players. |
| DVD-RW | Writable and rewritable (also called an erasable) version of the standard DVD-R or DVD-ROM. |
| DVD+R | Write-once disc that has some advantages over the DVD-R format but not as widely used and not compatible with a standard DVD player. |
| DVD+RW | Writable and rewritable version of the DVD+R standard, sharing that specification's advantages and incompatibility. |
| DVD-RAM | Original writable DVD format, not in wide use and compatible only with its own drives. |

Today, the competing DVD+ and DVD- makers have a truce; most modern laptops capable of writing or rewriting discs are hybrid devices that can work with each design. Look for a label that says DVD +/- R or RW. And you'll find many modern laptops offered with combination drives that are capable of working with both CDs and DVDs, or CDs and DVD-R/DVD-RWs.

Here's what *generally* works with what; test your laptop to be sure your particular model follows widely accepted rules.

| Device | Works With |
|---|---|
| CD-ROM | CD<br>Certain CD-R discs recorded on other machines |
| CD-R | CD<br>CD-R discs recorded on that machine and certain CD-R discs recorded on other machines<br>Certain CD-RW discs recorded on other machines |
| CD-RW | CD<br>CD-R discs recorded on that machine and certain CD-R discs recorded on other machines<br>CD-RW discs recorded on that machine and certain CD-RW discs recorded on other machines |
| DVD-ROM | DVD |
| DVD-R | DVD<br>DVD-R |
| DVD-RW | DVD<br>DVD-R<br>DVD-RW |
| DVD+RW | DVD<br>DVD+R<br>DVD+RW |

| Device | Works With |
|---|---|
| DVD +/- RW | DVD<br>DVD+R<br>DVD-R<br>DVD+R<br>DVD-R |
| CD-RW/DVD-ROM | CD<br>CD-R discs recorded on that machine and certain CD-R discs recorded on other machines<br>CD-RW discs recorded on that machine and certain CD-RW discs recorded on other machines<br>DVD |
| DVD +/-RW | CD<br>CD-R<br>CD-R discs recorded on that machine and certain CD-R discs recorded on other machines<br>CD-RW discs recorded on that machine and certain CD-RW discs recorded on other machines<br>DVD<br>DVD-R<br>DVD+R<br>DVD-RW<br>DVD+RW |

# Blu-ray Discs

Just when you thought you had a handle on the difference between a CD and a DVD, and the distinction between R and RW and -R and +R, along comes the latest and greatest form of optical storage: *Blu-ray (BD)*.

Once again, computer users are the beneficiaries of technology first developed for the wider consumer entertainment market. As *HD (high-definition)* TVs began taking a large portion of the market, movie studios and other "content" providers needed a way to deliver the huge amount of information required for HD equipment. Very quickly it became obvious that a basic 4.7GB DVD didn't have enough space for a full-length movie plus extras in high definition.

And so two groups of manufacturers began work on competing technologies. One was the HD DVD group, led by Toshiba, which came up with a design for a disc that could hold 15GB on a single layer or 30GB on a proposed dual-layer device. And the other, primarily backed by Sony, was the Blu-ray disc, which can hold 25GB on a single layer or 50GB on dual-layer drives. In a short but intense battle of the standards, Blu-ray came out on top; in early 2008, the HD DVD group threw in the towel.

Blu-ray discs have the same physical dimensions as a standard DVD or CD. The primary difference is the use of a blue-violet laser for reading and writing data; light of this color has a shorter wavelength of 405 nanometers, less than ⅔ that of the red laser (650nm) used on DVDs and a bit less than ½ of the 780nm red laser employed by CD writers. By decreasing the wavelength of the laser it became possible to make even tinier marks, and to stuff much more information onto the disc. The other technical hurdle was to develop a super-hard coating to protect the surface of the densely packed disc.

For laptop users this means storing and retrieving massive amounts of data, as much as 50GB, on a single removable disc. And not just data, either; since most laptop LCDs are already high definition, this means using your machine for entertainment as well. (Imagine that!)

The first Blu-ray drives began arriving in laptops in 2008. Because the discs are physically the same as older optical discs, manufacturers offer combination drives with multiple lasers that can work with Blu-ray as well as older DVD and CD media.

## Ejecting and Inserting a CD, DVD, or BD

The lightweight miniaturized optical drives used in laptops are stripped-down versions (in size and weight, not capability) of the devices found in desktop computers and home entertainment systems. One thing you generally *won't* find is a motorized drawer that slides open or closed; instead the drive is generally spring loaded. When you press a button near the drawer, it pops open; to close the drive, *gently* push it with your finger until it latches.

Laptop drives have a central spindle that includes the laser itself. Place the disc on the spindle and while supporting the drawer from the underside, gently push the disc into place. Install the disc with the label or printed side up.

Never force the disc onto the spindle and never force the drawer into the laptop; if something feels wrong, something *is* wrong.

Many programs automatically eject the drawer when you complete an operation (such as writing or rewriting a disc) or issue a software command to eject the disc.

If the drive drawer doesn't open in response to a software command or to pushing the button on the side of the laptop, you can *gently* engage a manual release; look for a pin-sized hole on the face of the drive. Straighten out a paper clip and carefully push it into the hole to open the drawer. See Figure 5-3.

**Figure 5-3**

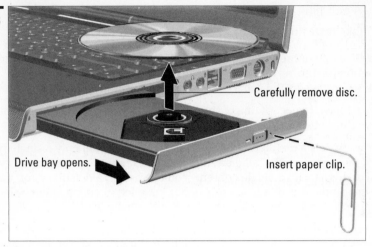

Carefully remove disc.

Drive bay opens.

Insert paper clip.

Courtesy of Hewlett-Packard Company

# Getting to AutoPlay

When you insert most (but not all) CDs, DVDs, or BDs into a read or read/write device on a laptop, Windows offers a dialog box of choices for appropriate actions; it's called AutoPlay.

For example, if you insert an audio disc into a CD player, the computer may offer to play songs from that media using Windows Media Player. If you insert an unformatted, blank disc, the computer may (quite logically) assume that you want to format and store data on it.

## Assigning AutoPlay

Anytime you insert a disc (or most other types of removable media, including flash memory keys), a dialog box suggests actions *if you haven't yet assigned a default AutoPlay action.*

For example, if you insert an optical disc that holds image files, the suggested actions on a Windows XP machine would include options like these:

- Copy pictures to my computer, using the Scanner and Camera Wizard.
- Open folder to view files, using Windows Explorer.
- Print the pictures, using Photo Printing Wizard.

    ✔ View a slide show of the images, using Windows Picture and Fax Viewer.

    ✔ Take no action.

If you click one of the suggested options and then click OK, Windows performs that action for the current disc, but you'll see the same options screen again the next time you insert the same or a similar device.

You don't have to accept one of the suggestions; just click the Cancel button to remove the AutoPlay dialog box.

Windows makes a distinction between discs that contain only a single type of file (all images, all audio, all data) and those that contain a mixture of types. For a disc or media with a single content, you can assign a default action that takes place each time this or a similar device is installed in your system: Select the Always Do the Selected Action checkbox, and then click OK.

Once you've assigned a default action, you'll no longer see the options screen. However, if you're running Windows Vista or Windows XP Service Pack 1 or later, if you install a new application that can also perform actions with the particular media type, the dialog box appears again so you can make a new selection.

Some applications ask if you want them to be identified as the default selection when they're installed; others may boorishly automatically claim that right. Discs that have mixed content present a similar dialog box of options, customized based on the available software in your system, but you aren't offered the option to set a default action, since the mixture may be different each time it's presented.

## Turning off AutoPlay

You can also instruct Windows not to offer AutoPlay suggestions; if you turn this feature off, you'll have to use My Computer or another Windows dialog box to see the contents of the disc or other media. You can also open an application (a word processor, an image editor, an audio player or editor) and navigate to the media using Open and a pull-down address bar.

Windows Vista users have a centralized place to control their laptops' AutoPlay functions for nearly every type of media or device that might be plugged into the machine (including BD, CD, or DVD discs holding audio, video, or digital images). You can tell the laptop what to do when it senses a blank optical disc. You can also instruct the operating system what to do if you plug a flash memory key into a USB port.

If you're running Windows Vista, to open the Autoplay menu take one of the following steps:

    *1.* Click the Windows button and type Autoplay into the search box.

    *2.* In the Programs panel, find AutoPlay and click it.

Or do this:

1. Click the Windows button and choose Control Panel.

2. Locate the AutoPlay item and click it.

Once the Vista AutoPlay program is displayed, use the pull-down arrows to make choices for each type of device found on your laptop.

Windows XP users can turn off AutoPlay by opening the removable drive's Properties dialog box:

1. Click the My Computer icon on the desktop.

2. Right-click the icon for the removable drive.

3. Choose Properties from the pop-up menu.

4. Click the AutoPlay tab.

5. Choose Select an Action to Perform.

6. Choose Take No Action.

7. Click OK.

TIP

To temporarily suspend AutoPlay, press the Alt key while loading the disc.

# Memories of Floppy and Flash Memory Drives

The oldest form of removable storage for personal computers is the floppy disk drive, now a rare item on a PC or laptop. One of the newest forms is the flash memory drive.

Although they're completely different when it comes to design and mechanical attributes, as far as you're concerned, they're very similar.

First the differences:

✔ A floppy disk drive uses a spinning, malleable platter of plastic that has a coating that holds a magnetic charge. The drive, about the size of two packs of playing cards alongside each other, contains two motors — one to spin the disk and a second to move the read/write head, picking up the notations or putting down new ones anywhere on the disk.

✔ Although larger-capacity floppy drives have been developed, nearly all PCs and laptops standardized on a specification called *high density (HD),* which packed a modest 1.44MB on a 3.5" disk within a plastic carrier.

✔ A flash memory drive has no moving parts and requires only a connecting point (a USB port) on the laptop. It contains a block of nonvolatile RAM that can hold data without the need for electrical power.

✔ When flash memory *keys* or *sticks* were first introduced, they offered a relatively paltry amount of storage (beginning at about 16MB of capacity), but today's models offer as much as 16GB.

With either type of device, though, a Windows system automatically recognizes a new disk or memory key; through Autoplay, Windows automatically opens a utility or program to access the information or offers choices.

You must format both devices before use. In formatting, the computer lays down an index and a grid of reference points so that it can find particular locations to store or retrieve information. Formatting a floppy disk drive usually takes one to two minutes; the much-larger capacity flash memory key requires only a fraction of that time.

AutoPlay may automatically detect that a newly installed device hasn't been formatted and offer to perform that action.

## Formatting a floppy disk

A manual route to formatting (or reformatting to remove existing files) works like this:

1. Insert the floppy disk into its drive.

2. Open the My Computer (Windows XP) or Computer (Windows Vista) icon on the Desktop.

3. Select Drive A:.

4. Right-click the device's icon and choose Format. Or, choose File⇨Format.

5. Choose one of these options:

   • Quick Format: Merely clears the index of existing files and makes space available for new files.

   • Full Format or Create an MS-DOS Startup Disk: Performs a more thorough cleaning and also adds the System Tracks that permit the floppy to be used as an emergency boot device.

6. Click the Start button.

   You may see a dialog box warning that you're about to irretrievably erase any data that is on the disk. (This isn't quite true, but nevertheless, you should stop and think before proceeding: Are you sure you want to clear this disk?)

7. Click the OK button.

## Formatting a flash memory key

Format (or reformat to remove existing files) manually, like this:

1. Insert a memory key into a USB port.

2. Click the My Computer (Windows XP) or Computer (Windows Vista) icon on the Desktop.

3. Select the drive letter for the flash memory key.

   That may be E: or higher on many machines.

4. Perform one of these:

   - Right-click the device's icon and choose Format.

   - Choose File⇨Format.

5. Click the Start button.

   You may see a dialog box warning that you're about to irretrievably erase any data that is on the disk. (This isn't quite true, but nevertheless, you should stop and think before proceeding: Are you sure you want to clear this disk?)

6. Click the OK button.

# *Undeleting and Unformatting*

Despite the warnings you get from Windows and certain instruction manuals, for-matting a drive or a memory key doesn't physically erase data from the medium. Instead, the index of filenames is changed so that when you use the device later, the system is unaware that there'd been a file in a particular spot. When you record new information to a previously used formatted drive, you're overwriting the old.

For most people that's good enough, but here's something to think about: With a capable software utility and just a bit of technical background, you (or an out-sider) can "undelete" or "unformat" almost any media that hasn't been overwrit-ten with new material. And even if a file has been partially covered over with new data, fragments may be accessible. Think about that before you throw away or give away an old floppy, an old flash memory key, or an old hard disk drive. And some might also worry about the possibility of theft of memory or its seizure by police or courts or unidentified men in black.

If this warning piques your personal paranoia, you might want to obtain and use a disk *scrubber* or *shredder*. These utilities overwrite specific files or an entire device with 0s or 1s; for optimum protection they sometimes write and rewrite gibberish several times.

# Folders, Subfolders, and Directories

If you're an organized person, you'll feel right at home using a computer running Windows. At the heart of the *operating system (OS)* is a logical structure of folders, subfolders, and directories. If you're not very organized, Windows stands ready to help you — if you take the time to find out how to use its folder system.

## In this part . . .

- ✔ Making folders smaller
- ✔ Customizing folders

# *Adventures in Windows Explorer*

One of the OS's unifying components is Windows Explorer, which displays folders, subfolders, and files in an almost unlimited variety of organizational schemes.

You can display Windows Explorer a number of ways:

- ✔ Locate a folder on the desktop and double-click to open it.

- ✔ Click the Windows button (in Windows Vista) or the Start button (in Windows XP), and then choose All Programs⇨Accessories⇨ Windows Explorer.

- ✔ Press the Windows key and choose one of the folders shown there.

- ✔ Press the key combination ⊞+E to display the My Computer or Computer screen and choose a folder.

- ✔ Under Windows Vista, click the Windows button and then type **Windows Explorer** into the search box. Click the utility name when it appears at the top of the menu.

Under Windows Vista, there is a built-in search box in all screens of Windows Explorer. You can type in the name of a file or program and the system will search for it and tell you its location; clicking on a filename will bring you to it.

## Customizing Windows Explorer under XP

You can decide what Windows displays in the left pane alongside the icons. Instruct the system to show additional information by clicking View⇨Toolbars; choose what you want to display.

You can call forth several of the windows with keyboard shortcuts when Windows Explorer is shown:

| *Window* | *What You Get* | *Shortcut from Windows Explorer* |
|---|---|---|
| Folders | The full structure of folders and subfolders on the current disk, and important system windows such as My Computer, My Network Places, and Recycle Bin. | — |
| Search | Broad or narrow searches for files, folders, computers, or people. | Ctrl+E or ⊞+E |

| Window | What You Get | Shortcut from Windows Explorer |
|--------|--------------|--------------------------------|
| Favorites | Your favorites, identified from within Internet Explorer or Windows Explorer, allowing a jump to a location on your hard drive or the Internet. | Ctrl+I or ⊞+I |
| History | The computer keeps track of the places you've navigated to (within your own system, the network, and the Internet) for the current day and as far back as 100 days ago, depending on browser settings. | Ctrl+H or ⊞+H |

History is a great way to find that place you accidentally stumbled across on the web, or that file — or forgotten name — you worked on yesterday.

Some users, though, worry about the availability of this information to others; you can clear the history from within Internet Explorer by clicking on Tools to display the menu and then choosing Internet Options. From the General tab, click the Clear History button. Note that you'll also find on the same tab the setting for number of days to keep pages in history.

## A tree with the root on top

Folders in Windows have a logical structure, even though the labels require a few twists and turns for a human to visualize. The *root* folder is the drive's top surface, outside of the folders. If you're talking about the first hard drive in a laptop, the root folder is most likely C:.

From this root folder sprout a dozen or a hundred or a thousand *trees*. The trees start with a folder on the desktop and then branch out, from the general to the increasingly specific. In computerspeak, the trees are said to go "down" from the desktop. Below the top folder is a series of *subfolders*. The Vista and XP versions of the folder are nearly identical; Vista, of course, is prettier. See Figure 6-1.

When you examine a tree in the navigation pane of Windows Explorer or any of its related windows (including My Documents, My Music, My Pictures, and My Network Places) or within the Open Files window of most applications, you see the root folder plus the top level of folders.

If any folder has one or more subfolders, you also see a plus symbol alongside. Click the plus to *expand* the display of that folder to the next sublevel; once it appears, click the minus symbol to *collapse* the display up a level.

**Figure 6-1**

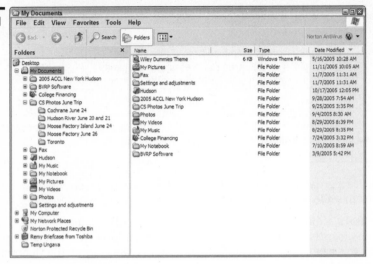

You can also use the keyboard to work your way through the tree. Use the Tab key to enter into the list, and then move as follows.

| Key | Action |
| --- | --- |
| ↑, ↓ | Move up or down in the list of folders |
| ← | Move left, or open a closed branch |
| → | Move right, or close an open branch |
| + | Open a branch (without moving the pointer) |
| - | Close a branch (without moving the pointer) |
| * | Open all branches |

Finally, you can also move from location to location on your hard drive, on network devices, or the Internet by typing directions in the *address bar.* If the address bar isn't already displayed, click View⇨Toolbars⇨Address Bar.

If you're using Windows Vista, and the menu bar — the one that includes the Tools and View menus — is invisible, type Alt+T.

# Compressing Folders

*Compressed folders* use mathematical and logical tricks to squeeze 10 pounds of stuff into a 5-pound bag, or more precisely something like 10MB of data in a 5-MB folder. The trick involves formulas (called *algorithms*) that look for repetitive characters or numbers that can be replaced with shorter blocks of data.

Compression works especially well with image or sound files. For example, say you had a picture of the front cover of this book. Large sections are made up of nothing more than blank yellow or black background. The computer's file describing the cover might start with 10,000 iterations of the 24-bit binary code 111111111111111100000000, which is equivalent to the hexadecimal code FFFF00 (system code for yellow) to describe just the first 10 rows of data from the top. An uncompressed image file, then, might have to use up 240,000 bits (about 30,000 bytes) just to describe those first 10 lines.

But say you used a compression program that analyzed those 240,000 identical bits and instead wrote a description that said: $10,000 \times 111111111111111100000000$. That instruction might take up just 32 bits of space.

One important detail: You need to use the same algorithm to compress and decompress the file. Everything else is handled by the extremely fast computer.

In the early days of personal computing and laptops, hard disk drives were measured in megabytes rather than gigabytes and space was at a premium. And users didn't have large recordable CDs or huge recordable DVDs to offload files. Older technologies for transmitting files, including dial-up modems, also benefited from any compression; smaller files take less time to transmit than larger ones. Today, high-speed broadband and WiFi networks make that less of an issue.

However, compressed folders and files are still valuable. With Windows XP, compressed files became fully integrated into the OS after being generated previously by third-party add-on programs.

## Creating a compressed folder

There are several ways to make a compressed folder:

- ✔ On the desktop, right-click and choose New⇨Compressed (zipped) Folder.
- ✔ From Windows Explorer, choose File⇨New⇨Compressed (zipped) Folder.

The icon for a compressed file looks just like a regular file, except that it has a little zipper on it.

## Adding files to a compressed folder

You can add files to a compressed folder in much the same way you'd add them to a regular folder:

- ✔ Drag and drop files from one folder to the compressed folder.

- ✔ Copy and paste from one folder to another.

- ✔ Select one or more files and then choose File⇨Send To⇨Compressed (Zipped) Folder to send files to an existing compressed folder.

Not allowed: a command to Move This File or Copy This File.

## Extracting files from a compressed folder

In most applications, you can't directly open or work with a compressed file. Instead the file must be *extracted* or *decompressed*. Follow along to extract a file:

1. Open the compressed folder.

2. Select a single file or a group of files.

3. From the File and Folder tasks pane, choose one option:

   - Copy This File

   - Move This File

To extract all the files in a compressed folder, choose File⇨Extract All. The files are decompressed and placed in a folder with the same name as the compressed folder, but without the zipper.

## Password protection for compressed folders

Unique among Windows folders, a compressed folder can be protected by a password. Locking the folder within a password is easy:

1. Open the compressed folder window.

2. Choose File⇨Add a Password.

The hard part: If you forget the password for compressed folders, the files within are as good as gone. Microsoft offers no tools to unlock a password-protected compressed folder. You may find some help in the murky world of password-cracker utilities. You may find some third-party utilities that offer to add password protection to any folder, and some that promise to unlock password-protected compressed folders. Proceed at your own risk.

# Designing Folders

You can customize many of the features of Windows folders, including appearance and behavior. The key to the settings is found in the Control Panel.

You can display folder options two ways:

- ✓ Open the Control Panel and click the Folder Options icon.

- ✓ From within any Windows Explorer window (including Windows Explorer, My Documents, My Music, and My Pictures under Windows XP or Documents, Music, Pictures, and other folders under Windows Vista), choose Tools⇨ Folder Options. The version of the Folder Options panel shown in Figure 6-2 is from Windows Vista and includes some additional customization choices.

**Figure 6-2**

The General tab controls how folders behave. The tab has three sections, or *panes:*

- ✓ Tasks determines whether a task pane appears in a folder window (the standard Windows XP settings) or whether no task pane is shown (the so-called Windows Classic scheme).

- ✓ Browse Folders controls whether a new window opens each time you open a new folder.

- ✓ Click Items as Follows instructs the system whether folders and files open with a single click or double-click.

If you have the folder set up to require a double-click, then the first click will select the item and the second click opens it up.

The View tab (see Figure 6-3) controls whether certain types of files and folders are displayed, and how much information is reported. Among the more important of the two dozen or so advanced settings are whether

🖛 The system automatically searches for available network folders and printers.

🖛 The contents of System folders are displayed.

🖛 The full path to a file or folder is displayed in the address bar or the title bar.

🖛 Hidden files and folders are displayed.

🖛 All filename extensions are displayed along with filenames or icons.

**Figure 6-3**

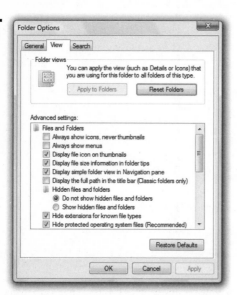

## Customizing the Appearance of a Folder

You can choose to add an image that sits on the front panel of the electronic file folder, change the icon for the folder from office stationery to something more indicative of its contents, or apply a folder template. See Figure 6-4.

**Figure 6-4**

## Adding a picture to a folder

To put a picture on the folder icon, do the following:

1.  Right-click the folder you want to accessorize.

2.  From the pop-up menu, choose Properties.

3.  Click the Customize tab.

4.  Click the Folder pictures button in Windows Vista.

    Or click the Choose Pictures button in Windows XP.

5.  Use the Browse dialog box to locate an image on your laptop or on an attached network device.

6.  Click the Open button to select the image.

7.  Click the OK button.

To remove a previously placed image, click the Restore Default button.

## Changing a folder's icon

To change the icon for a folder from an electronic version of a manila sleeve to another icon included in the set supplied with Windows (or to an image of your own) do this:

1. Right-click the folder you want to change.

2. From the pop-up menu, choose File⇨Properties.

3. Click the Customize tab.

4. Click the Change Icon button.

5. Browse the Change Icon dialog box to locate a replacement icon on your hard drive or on an attached network device.

6. Click OK twice.

### Assigning a template to a folder

Windows Vista and Windows XP include a set of templates for certain types of files; these offer customized sets of commands that match collections of images, music, or text. To apply a template to a folder, do this:

1. Right-click the folder you want to change.

2. From the pop-up menu, choose File⇨Properties.

3. Click the Customize tab.

4. In the top pane, locate Use This Type as a Template. Click the down arrow and choose a folder type. A typical selection includes the following:

   • Documents (for any file type)

   • Pictures (best for many files)

   • Picture Album (best for fewer files)

   • Music (best for audio files and playlists)

   • Music Artist (best for works by one artist)

   • Music Album (best for tracks from one album)

   • Videos

5. Click the OK button.

## Managing Folders

Folders can be acted on in much the same way as files. You can create, delete, rename, copy, and move files. Just remember that a folder bulging with files could present a major problem if it's misplaced, misnamed, or somehow damaged.

## Creating a new folder

On the Windows Desktop or within any open folder in your system, perform one of the following steps:

- ✔ Right-click and choose New⇨Folder.
- ✔ Click File⇨New⇨Folder.

The system creates the folder and gives it a generic name like *New Folder*. The name is automatically selected, and you can rename by typing in a title from the keyboard.

## Deleting a folder and its contents

To delete a folder, follow these steps:

1. Click to select the folder.
2. Perform one of the following steps:
   - • Right-click and choose Delete.
   - • Click File⇨Delete.
   - • Press the Delete key on the keyboard.

When you delete a folder, the container and all of its contents are removed. Take care not to delete a folder containing programs and Windows components; these are ordinarily removed using special Uninstall utilities accessible from the Control Panel or from the programs themselves.

When a folder is deleted, it's ordinarily placed in the Recycle Bin and can be recovered from there if it hasn't worked its way to the top of the pile and been overwritten. Note, though, that some files or folders are too large to reside in the Recycle Bin and, if deleted, are inaccessible using that utility.

## Renaming a folder

Renaming a folder follows the same procedures you use to give a new name to a file. Perform one of the following steps:

- ✔ Right-click a folder name, then choose Rename.
- ✔ Click File⇨Rename.
- ✔ Click a folder name (not the icon), pause, then click once more on the name.
- ✔ Click a folder name, then press the F2 key.

Once you've selected the folder name, type in a new name. As with filenames, you can use upper- and lowercase characters in a folder name for your own purposes, but the system doesn't distinguish between cases when it comes to using the folders.

## Copying or moving a folder

You can drag and drop folders from one location to another; the files within travel with the folder.

Follow these steps to copy a file:

1. Click the file to select it.

2. Do one of these two things:

   - Choose Edit⇨Copy to make a second version of the folder and its contents.

   - Choose Edit⇨Cut to copy the folder and its contents to the clipboard.

   The keyboard equivalents of these two commands are Ctrl+C for copy and Ctrl+X for cut.

3. Go to the folder's new location.

   It can be the desktop or any other folder, including Windows Explorer.

4. Choose Edit⇨Paste.

   This copies the folder and its contents (or pastes the folder if the process began with Edit⇨Cut). The keyboard equivalent to paste a file is Ctrl+V.

## Creating a shortcut to a folder

Instead of moving or copying a file, you can create a shortcut to it and put the shortcut on the desktop or in any other folder.

To create a shortcut, follow these steps:

1. Click a file.

2. Choose Edit⇨Copy.

3. Navigate to the shortcut location and choose Edit⇨Paste Shortcut.

You can accomplish the same steps by doing one of these:

- Right-clicking a file, selecting Copy, navigating to a new location, right-clicking again, and selecting Paste Shortcut.

- Right-clicking a file or folder, choosing Create Shortcut, and then moving the shortcut to where you want it.

- Choosing Send to⇨Desktop (create shortcut).

# *Files*

A computer file is the electronic equivalent of a sheaf of papers, stapled together to keep them from straying, and given a label so you can find them again. That definition says nothing about the quality of the information on those papers and makes no claim about whether the contents are organized, categorized, logical, or in any way worthwhile. That part of the equation is up to you.

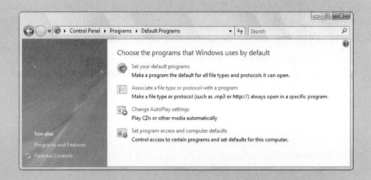

## In this part . . .

- ✓ **Opening a file in a certain program**
- ✓ **Looking for missing files**
- ✓ **Naming, renaming, and moving files**

# *Dissecting a File*

A text file may contain illiterate and indecipherable gibberish or the unpublished manuscript of the next bestselling novel. An image file may hold a childish scribble or a fabulous photo. A file may contain a program or the settings for that software.

The other thing to keep in mind is that the file, like everything else within the computer, is made up of simple binary code: 0s and 1s. Everything is reduced to a number, from the value of a character in text to whether a particular dot is turned on or off in an image displayed on-screen or sent to a printer.

Content begins in the computer's memory; if you turn off the laptop before the data is saved as a file, the content disappears like the fading glow of a lamp when power is shut off.

Files provided by a software maker arrive with their own names and other components already in place. Files you create on your own machine generally need to be given a name and a type; nearly all software programs apply a default name and file type when you save your work. If you disagree with the name, file type, and intended location within your laptop, you must make changes on your own.

These details are quite important. The filename helps you keep track of what lies within, while filename extensions and associated file types help the computer determine which software application is designed to work with the contents. These labels are called file *attributes*.

## Filename

A filename provides a recognizable identity. In the earliest versions of the PC operating system, names could be no more than 8 characters long. Under current Windows versions including Vista, names can be as long as 260 characters, including letters, numbers, spaces, and many of the symbols available on the keyboard. Keep in mind, though, that the limit of 260 characters includes the complete path to the location of the file. So, for example, if the file is at C:\My_Documents\Dummies\Laptops_Quick_Reference\Second_Edition\, whatever filename you create begins with a 63-character head start.

And anyhow, even though you can use names long enough for a complete sentence, you'll probably find it easier to track your files by limiting them to no more than about 25 characters. The following characters are among those that *aren't* permitted in filenames:

* / \ : " ? | < >

Spaces are permitted in filenames, although they can sometimes cause confusion to humans looking for them. As an alternative, you can place underscores between words, as in My_Sample_File.

You can use either lowercase or uppercase letters if it makes it easier for you to recognize the file. For example, you can call a file This_is_My_Resume if you'd like. However, internally, Windows pays no attention to the case of letters and therefore you cannot have another file called THIS_is_MY_resume in the same location.

The best plan is to adopt a consistent naming scheme; for example, each of the files I wrote for this book began with a code that identified them by project followed by a chapter number and a subject, as in 240564 LAP_DUMMIES_QR Chap05 Files. No one scheme is right or wrong, but if it makes no sense to you when you want to find a file days, weeks, months, or years later, find another scheme.

## Icon

Icons are the tiny pictures applied to files under Windows and are a graphical version of the filename extension and its associated file type. Most Windows applications automatically associate an icon with files created within that program; later in this chapter you explore how to change the association of a particular program to a file.

## File size

Size is indicated in number of bytes or characters within the file. In My Documents and Open boxes of Windows, the size is rounded up to the nearest kilobyte or megabyte. You can see the exact size by highlighting its name or icon, right-clicking, and then choosing Properties from the pop-up menu.

## File creation date

The file creation date is when the file was first created and saved.

## File modified date

The most recent date when the file was altered is the file modified date.

## Attributes

Files can be marked as *read-only* (can't be modified and saved under the same name), *hidden* (not displayed in files lists), or other indicators, including the fact that they've been backed up to another location since the last modification.

## Filename extension

The last part of a filename, separated from it by a period, helps tie a file to the program that created it or to a group of programs able to work with a particular type of file. You can usually assign an extension by putting one in place when you name it; in most instances, though, a software program adds the extension automatically or when you choose a file type in a dialog box.

Check out these common filename extensions and their meanings. (Hundreds of others exist; you can usually find out their meaning by searching on the Internet.)

| Extension | Meaning |
| --- | --- |
| .BMP | A bitmap image file, a low-resolution specification for pictures, icons, and photos used on web sites and in some other on-screen applications. |
| .COM | A command file, a form of program. |
| .DOC | A word-processing document, usually Microsoft Word, although other editors may be able to open and work with these files. |
| .DOCX | A newer form of document storage for Word documents introduced with Office 2007; such XML files are typically smaller and more resistant to corruption than earlier formats. |
| .EXE | An executable file, a form of program. |
| .GIF | A general image format, a specification that requires relatively less storage size for images and icons primarily because it limits the total palette of colors to 256. |
| .HTM | A hypertext markup language file with instructions for displaying a page online. Also can be .html. |
| .JPG | An image format developed by the Joint Photographic Experts Group, JPEGS use compression to reduce file size. |
| .MID | A musical instrument digital interface file designed to provide digital instructions to a MIDI instrument. |
| .MPG | An audio file that follows the specification of the Moving Pictures Expert Group, MPEGS compress video files. Also can be .MPEG. |
| .PDF | Portable Document Format, developed for use with Adobe Acrobat and compatible products; files can deliver images, animation, text, and sound. |
| .PIF | A Program Information File that contains identifying data for use by drivers that bridge the gap between the operating system and the specific pieces of hardware in a computer. Used primarily in Windows XP and earlier operating systems; Windows Vista handles these files in a different manner. |
| .PPT | A Microsoft PowerPoint document. |
| .PPTX | A newer form of document storage for PowerPoint documents introduced with Office 2007; such XML files are typically smaller and more resistant to corruption than earlier formats. |
| .RTF | Rich Text Format, a specification for a word-processing file with formatting that isn't specific to an editor. |
| .TIF | A Tagged Image File Format, an image storage specification that doesn't compress or otherwise degrade data. |
| .TXT | Plain text from an editor or word processor, without formatting for fonts, margins, and other niceties. |

| Extension | Meaning |
| --- | --- |
| .WAV | A waveform audio file, used for many sound files on a computer. |
| .XLS | A Microsoft Excel worksheet. |
| .XLSX | A newer form of document storage introduced with Office 2007 for Microsoft Excel worksheets; such XML files are typically smaller and more resistant to corruption than earlier formats. |
| .ZIP | A file that's been compressed by using WinZip or PKZip; files don't lose any information in the shrinking process. |

## Reading a file's details

You can check on a file's many attributes by using the Windows Explorer program. The standard display is automatically fitted to the type of files within a particular folder. In addition, you can customize which attributes are shown.

The first decision is how you want to view your files:

✔ Icons

✔ Simple list of filenames

✔ Detailed list of filenames with information

To learn the most about your files in the most efficient manner, click Views⇨Details when you're looking at a folder of files.

As an example, a Windows Explorer display of images can include attributes such as name, size, type, date modified, attributes, owner, camera model, date picture taken, and dimensions. (Attributes in this listing refer to whether a particular file has been archived to a backup file, is a hidden or invisible file, or is a read-only document.)

To show a list of available details, right-click any column header already in use. This brings up a list of details; click to select or deselect individual categories. See Figure 7-1.

You can also customize the appearance of the details in the window. Here are some options:

✔ Sort files based on any column. For example, to list files in alphabetical order based on name, click the Name header. Click again to sort in reverse order.

✔ Change column sequence. Click and drag a header left or right.

✔ Adjust column width. Click and drag the right edge of the heading; drag it right to expand, and left to contract.

✔ Adjust a column to be wide enough for its widest item. Double-click the right edge of a column header to make this adjustment.

**Figure 7-1**

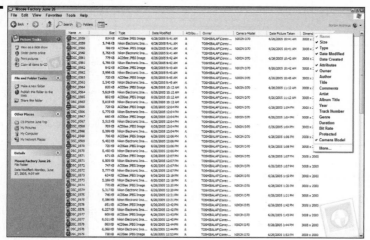

For the greatest flexibility, select the displayed data set by instructing the system you want to Choose Details. Here's how to reach this somewhat buried treasure:

1. Go to a Windows Explorer page, accessible through My Documents, My Pictures, My Music, and other Windows displays.

2. Right-click a header and choose More.

3. Select or deselect details to display or hide them.

   Use the slider on the right side of the screen to show more detail options. (You can't deselect Name; if you suppressed the filename, you can't select the file.)

4. Highlight a detail with the pointer, and click Move Up or Move Down to change column order.

 You can manually assign the width of individual columns by highlighting one and entering a pixel value. You may have to experiment to get the proper value for your screen size and resolution.

5. Click OK and close the Windows Explorer screen.

 To get to Choose Details in Windows Vista, you may need to display the Classic menu bar.

1. Open a Windows Explorer page.

2. Press and release the Alt key.

3. Click Tools➪Choose Details. See Figure 7-2.

**Figure 7-2**

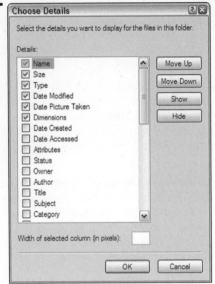

**Reading a file's properties**

You can also find a great deal of information about individual files by right-clicking the filename and choosing Properties.

At the top of the Properties screen you see the filename; you can make a change here. (Some applications don't permit changing the file if it's already open in a program. And keep in mind that this is the equivalent of the Save As command, meaning that you end up with two copies: the original and a new file with the same contents but a new name.)

You'll see the file type, an identification set by one or more of the following:

- ✔ A filename extension that's automatically linked to a particular application.

- ✔ A filename extension that's been latched onto by a particular program as part of its installation program. For example, an image editor may unilaterally declare ownership of all TIF or JPG files, at least when it comes to document-based file opening. (*Document based* means that a particular program loads when you open a particular file type.)

- ✔ A filename extension customized by you during the installation of the program or manually assigned when the file was saved. In the next section I explain how to change this association to a program.

Other Properties screen information includes the file's location on your hard drive. You often find that you can't read the full location for a file that has a long name, or one buried several subfolders deep on a drive; one solution is to hover (don't click) the mouse pointer over the Location name; Windows displays the full path to the location of the file in a bubble onscreen.

You'll also see the file size, in the computer shorthand of KB or MB, as well as an actual byte count. Remember that 1KB is equal to 1,024 bytes rather than an even (decimal-based) 1,000, so the larger the file, the greater the differential between KB or MB and the actual number of bytes. (As an example, a 1MB file is shown as containing 1,048,576 bytes.)

Next you see the size on disk, which is the space the file occupies on the storage medium. As part of the formatting process, all storage devices — hard disk drives, flash memory keys, CD or DVD discs, and anything else — divide space into *blocks,* or *sectors.* In general, the larger the overall amount of space, the larger the memory block. If that block is 512KB and your file contains 540KB (552,960 bytes), it will occupy two blocks. That's wasteful on a small drive and relatively insignificant on a large one.

Here's a real example of the strange math of file sizes and storage sizes. I'm looking at a Word file that's listed on the Properties pages as 89.0KB. Next to that number I see the actual number of bytes, which turns out to be 91,136, which is what you get when you multiply 89 times 1,024 to convert from binary math to decimal math. The next information is the size on disk, which is listed first as a nice, even 92.0KB; alongside that number I can see that this occupies 94,208 bytes in storage. The bottom line is that the file, as stored on my particular hard disk drive, requires the equivalent of an additional 3,072 bytes because of the way the drive is organized by block. By one way of reasoning, 89K equals 94,028 bytes.

Other file information on the Properties screen includes its creation date, last modification time, and the last access time. Finally, you can make the file read-only or hidden via a pair of checkboxes.

## Associating a File with a Program

Users of Windows Vista or Windows XP can easily instruct the operating system how to work with particular files or filenames. Here are the steps for Vista:

1. Click the Windows button, then click Computer.

2. Double-click a drive or folder, opening folders until the file you want to change is displayed.

3. Click a file and then right-click.

4. Choose Open With.

5. Choose the program you want to open when you click that file.

6. Click OK.

Another way to make a new file association: Click Choose Default Program. Then click Browse to find the new program you want to associate with the file. If you want all files with this particular filename extension to open with a particular program, click the Always Use the Selected Program to Open This Kind of File check box.

If you're using Windows XP, you can also use a Control Panel utility to associate a particular type of file with a specific program. To associate a filename extension with a file type, do the following:

1. Go to the Control Panel.

2. Double-click the Folder Options icon.

3. Click the File Types tab.

4. Click New.

5. From the keyboard, type in a new or existing filename extension.

6. Click Advanced.

7. Click the Associated File Type drop-down menu to display all the known file types in the system.

Also in Windows XP, follow these instructions to change the program that opens a file:

1. Go to the Control Panel.

2. Double-click the Folder Options icon.

3. Click the File Types tab.

4. Highlight an existing filename extension and its associated file type.

5. Click Change to open the Open With window.

6. Select a new association and click OK.

Windows Vista users can also set default programs through the Control Panel. In the advanced view, select Programs⇨Default Programs.

# *Launching a Search Party for a Missing File*

You're not alone: Almost everyone has lost or misplaced a file. Anyone who says otherwise has probably forgotten about the existence of a file they can't find.

The most common cause of a misplaced file is putting it in the wrong folder; the second most likely cause is an incorrect or misleading filename. (Perhaps the name made some sense when you created it.)

## Quick searching in Windows Vista

Here is an area where Windows Vista offers a significant advantage over Windows XP. Under Vista, if you click the Windows button (on-screen) or the Windows key (on your keyboard), you see an updated version of the Start menu that includes a box marked Start Search. Type in as much of the filename as you know, or a specific (and uncommon) word that you know is contained in a file.

Vista performs an on-the-fly indexing of files you create and can very quickly present you with a list of likely suspects. The more specific you are, the more likely you are to jump quickly and directly to its location.

## Detailed searching in Windows Vista and XP

The Windows XP search utility is quite capable, but in its standard configuration, the best way to find a misplaced file is to enlist the Windows Search utility.

Windows Vista users can also employ the Search utility. You can get to it two ways:

  ✔ Click the Start button and select Search.

  ✔ Go to any Windows Explorer screen (including My Computer, My Documents, My Music, and My Pictures) and press the F3 key.

To perform highly specific searches using Windows Vista, click the Advanced Search menu item. You can also reach the Search utility from any Windows Explorer screen (including Computer, Documents, Music, or Pictures) and then press the F3 key.

Windows XP users can bring up Search several ways:

  ✔ Click the Start button and select Search.

  ✔ Go to any Windows Explorer screen (including My Computer, My Documents, My Music, and My Pictures) and do one of the following:

   • Click the Search button.

   • Press the F3 key.

   • Press Ctrl+E.

   • Choose View➪Explorer Bar➪Search.

## Searching by name

If you know a missing file's exact name, or at least part of the name, you can narrow the scope of a search. Here's how:

1. Open the Search utility.

    Skip to Step 3 if you don't know the file type.

2. If you know the file type, select it. Your choices include

    • Pictures, music, or video

    • Documents (word processing, spreadsheet, and the like)

    • All files and folders

3. If you don't know the file type, select Choose All Files and Folders.

    If you know that the file held a .TIF or .MPG extension, you can cut down on the search by choosing the pictures, music, or video category; if you know it was created and saved by a word processor as a .DOC file, choose the documents category.

4. Enter data you're certain of in the All or Part of the File Name section.

    Shorten the search by limiting the places the computer looks. This is mostly a process of elimination. If you're certain that the file was stored on your single C: hard drive, specify that location. Other choices include any other attached storage device (including a floppy disk, a recordable CD or DVD disc, or other removable media).

5. Click the Search button.

6. If a file that meets your criteria is found, it appears in the right pane.

## Searching by contents

If you know a specific *unusual* word or phrase in a file, limit the search to the contents of files on the computer or attached to it. I say *unusual* because it makes no sense to search for commonplace words that are likely to be found in almost any file. But if you think you used a name (say, Philo Kvetch) in just a few pieces of work, then searching just for that may be the fastest way to locate the missing file.

1. Open the Search utility.

2. Select All Files and Folders.

3. Enter data in A Word or Phrase in the File section.

    Shorten the search by limiting the places where the computer will look.

4. Click the Search button.

### Searching by edit or creation date

You can sharply limit the number of searched files (and thus the time) by selecting a time period:

1. Open the Search utility.

2. Select All Files and Folders.

3. Enter data in one of these sections:

   • All or Part of the File Name

   • A Word or Phrase in the File

   Shorten the search by limiting the places where the computer will look.

4. Click the When Was It Modified? drop-down list and choose an option:

   • Within the last week

   • Past month

   • Within the past year

   • Specify dates

5. Click the Search button.

## Finding the Path to Your File

You can set up a virtually bottomless pit of folders and subfolders located on internal and external hard drives and removable media. That's the good news; the bad news is that it's sometimes difficult for a human (not the machine) to keep track of files.

The first part of the solution involves adopting a logical structure for your storage devices. It doesn't necessarily have to make sense to anyone else but you. For example, as a writer I've set up my main desktop computer (and my laptop, which serves as a traveling extension of the desktop) with this basic structure for files. See Figure 7-3.

**Figure 7-3**

```
My Documents
    Projects
        Computer books
            Dummies
                    Upgrading Laptops
                    Laptops Quick Reference
                Fix Your Own PC
                PC Upgrade
        Travel books
                Econoguide
        Business books
                Small business
                Performance Evaluation
        Fiction
    Archives
        Published books
        Financial backups
    Business
            Contracts
            Banking
            Investments
            Legal
    Personal
            Letters
            Resumes
            Medical
            Educational
```

The files for this very book you're reading reside in a subfolder called Laptops Quick Reference, which lies four levels below the My Documents folder on the desktop. If you charted out its location, you could use a notation called a computer *path*. The path to the file (under its working title of 05 Working with Files) could be written like this:

C:\Windows\Desktop\Projects\Computer Books\Dummies\Laptops Quick Reference\05 Working with Files.doc

The parts of the pathname follow:

- ✔ **Drive letter:** The computer's identifying letter for the physical storage device. On nearly all computers, the first internal hard drive is C, and a typical assignment for a CD or DVD drive is D, although other letters can be used.

- ✔ **Folder:** The first folder is called the *root* or *root folder*. In my example, the root folder is \Windows. On some systems the root folder exists outside Windows and has a different name.

- ✔ **Subfolder:** Folders that are *below* or within a higher-level folder are represented by a backslash followed by their name. For example, C:\Windows\Desktop is a subfolder of the root folder \Windows on drive C:.

- ✔ **Filename:** The final part of the pathname is the file itself, including a filename extension.

If your laptop is connected to a network, the drive letter may be replaced by a computer name. For example, if you call your desktop computer JOHN (as in a set named John, Paul, George, and Ringo), the file path on that machine might be this:

\\JOHN\Shared\California_Trip\itinerary.doc

The double backslash identifies the location as a network resource. Below that is a folder and a subfolder, followed by a filename.

# Managing Your Files

You are the master of your own domain, at least when it comes to the files you keep locally on your laptop. Among the tools at your command are Save, Copy, Move, Rename, Delete, and Undelete.

## Saving a file

All of your work exists only in the temporary memory (RAM) of your laptop until you instruct the computer to save a copy to a file in storage: on the hard drive, on a memory key, on a CD or DVD, or any other media.

Every Windows application includes a command to save files created with that program and most work in a similar manner. Here are the common ways to save a file:

- Click File⇨Save.

- Press Ctrl+S.

- Exit the program. Nearly every program stops before shutting down and offers the option to save any open files. If the file's already been saved and no changes have been made since then, the option isn't offered.

The first time you save a particular file, you're given the opportunity to name the file, choose a location other than the one the program suggests, and assign a file type.

You can take a free hand in your choice of name and location, but take care with file type. A poorly chosen type can affect formatting of a word-processing file and affect compatibility of any file with particular programs. Consult the help screens and instruction manuals for software for advice about file types.

## Choosing Save As

Once you've saved a file for the first time, you can later choose to make a copy of that file under a different name, in a different location, or as a changed file type. One way to do that is to use the Save As command.

Here's how:

1. Choose File⇨Save as.

2. In the File Name box, enter a name for the file.

   The name can be new, or you can use an existing name if you plan to place the file in a new location or save it as a different file type.

3. Click the Save as Type list and choose the file format you want to use for the file.

   If you make no change here, the file's saved in the same format it currently uses.

4. Under Windows XP, if you want to save the file in a location other than the one previously used or the one suggested by the system, click on a displayed subfolder or on the Up one level button to move to a different subfolder or folder.

In Windows Vista, to save the file somewhere other than where the system suggests, use the folder navigation pane or the address bar at the top of the window to select a new place.

## Copying a file

A copy is, as you'd expect, a duplicate version of the file. If it's in the same folder as the original, it must have a different name, but it can be as simple a change as *my sample textfile.doc* and *my sample textfile[2].doc* If the copy is stored elsewhere, or on removable media, it can have the same name.

You can copy a file a number of ways. Here are some of the most common.

To copy a file from Windows Explorer using menu commands, do the following:

1. From a Windows Explorer screen (including My Computer, My Documents, My Music, and My Pictures), highlight a file and right-click.

2. Select Copy.

3. Navigate to a new location from within the Windows Explorer Screen.

4. Right-click a blank spot of the list of files or icons on the location where you want the copy.

5. Select Paste.

To copy more than one file at a time, click the first item and then press and hold down the Shift key. Click the last item in a series of files to select all between the first and last. You can select nonconsecutive files by pressing and holding down the Ctrl key as you individually select items in a list of files.

You can copy from Windows Explorer by using keyboard commands to copy a file to the computer's clipboard (in its memory) and then pasting it. Here's how:

1. From a Windows Explorer screen (including My Computer, My Documents, My Music, and My Pictures), highlight a file.

2. Press Ctrl+C to copy the file to the clipboard.

3. Navigate to a new location from within the Windows Explorer Screen.

4. Click a blank spot of the list of files or icons on the location where you want the copy.

5. Press Ctrl+V to copy the file from the clipboard to the new location.

If you open two Windows Explorer screens and display them both, you can drag and drop files from one to the other, leaving the original where it was and creating a copy. Here's how:

1. Open a Windows Explorer screen and click folders until you're at the location of the file to be copied.

2. Open a second Windows Explorer screen and click folders (or create them) until you're where the copy is to be.

3. Ctrl+ drag the file to copy from its source to its destination, and then release the buttons.

   If you don't press and hold the Ctrl key, you'll *move* the file from one location to another instead of copying it.

Use this method to move from one folder to another, or from one drive to another.

## Duplicating a file

If you want to make an identical copy of a file in the same location as the original, do so by copying and pasting it.

Why would you want a duplicate? You may want to leave the original version of a file untouched while you make changes and additions to a copy, or you may want an original before applying special file formatting.

To duplicate, do this:

1. From a Windows Explorer screen (including My Computer, My Documents, My Music, and My Pictures), highlight a file and right-click.

2. Select the file to duplicate.

3. Choose Edit⇨Copy.

4. Choose Edit⇨Paste.

If the original filename was *sample text.doc*, the resulting duplicate copy is *Copy of sample text.doc*.

## Renaming a file

Files are named as you create them in Windows applications. If the program applies a name you don't like, if the contents of the file changes over time, or if for any other reason you want to change the name, do this:

1. Select the file or icon you want to rename.

2. Do one of the following actions:

   • Right-click and choose Rename.

   • Click the filename once. Don't double-click.

   • Press the F2 key.

3. Type a new name.

If Windows doesn't allow you to rename, it's probably because you've included illegal characters or attempted to give the same name as another file in the same location.

For details about allowable characters for a filename, see the section called "Labeling a file" earlier in this chapter.

## Moving a file

When you move a file, it is (in logical terms) deleted from its original location and re-created in its new location. That's exactly what happens if you're moving it from one storage device to another — from your hard drive to an external device.

But if you're merely moving a file from one folder on your hard drive to another, the computer doesn't actually delete and move it. Instead, it makes a change in the information in the drive's index. As a user, this makes no difference to you.

## Deleting a file

To delete a file, click its icon and then do one of the following:

- ✓ Press Delete.

- ✓ With the file highlighted, click File⇨ Delete.

- ✓ From a Windows Explorer screen on the desktop, click+drag the file to the Recycle Bin. Release the mouse button when the bin changes color or shade.

Some programs may display a warning asking if you really want to delete the file.

One more thing: When you "delete" most files, you're not really deleting them. Instead, you're causing them to be no longer displayed within Windows Explorer and ordinary Open File screens; they're in the Recycle Bin.

Files remain in the Recycle Bin until they work their way from the bottom (most recently deleted) to the top. While files are in the bin, you can undelete by double-clicking the icon. Files are finally deleted when they've aged; the time from arrival in the Recycle Bin to the departure depends on two factors: how much space you instruct the system to devote to it, and how many files you delete in a particular period.

If you want to delete a file without an intermediate rest stop in the Recycle Bin, click the file and press Shift+Delete.

## Undeleting a file

To restore a file that's still in the Recycle Bin, do the following:

1.  Double-click the Recycle Bin on the desktop.

2.  Choose View⇨Details to arrange items in columns.

*3.* Arrange the information so you can find the file.

- If you know the filename (or at least its first few characters), click the Name column.

- If you know when the file was deleted, click the Date Deleted column.

- If you know the file type (such as image, audio, or video), click the Type column.

*4.* Click the file you want to recover.

To highlight more than one contiguous file, press Shift and draw the mouse pointer up or down in a list. To highlight files that aren't contiguous, press Ctrl and click the files you want to recover.

*5.* Choose File⇨ Restore.

Some adaptations of the Recycle Bin, such as the Norton Protected Recycle Bin, have a Recover button just below the file list.

The Windows Vista version of the Recycle Bin is very similar, although it has a few differently named commands. If you highlight an individual file, you see Restore This Item. If you don't highlight any specific files, the same button reads Restore All Items. Choose the one that's most appropriate for you.

When you restore or recover a file, it is automatically returned to the folder it occupied when you deleted it. If there's another file with the same name, in most cases Windows renames the recovered file as a copy. After you restore a file, you can move it elsewhere on your computer.

# Networks

Networks are especially wonderful for laptops is that they fit perfectly with a laptop as an extension of your desktop. With a wireless network link, you can download mail, upload work, and research on the office database. A wired link from a laptop offers the same advantages, often at higher speed and greater security, when you plug into a network at a branch office, a client, or anywhere else with an available port.

## In this part . . .

- ↙ **Gathering the technology you need to network**
- ↙ **Naming and addressing a network**
- ↙ **Networking with wires and without**

# Assembling Networking Nuts and Bolts

Windows comes equipped with all the basic networking software most users need.

On the hardware side, you need the following:

- ✔ A *network interface card (NIC),* which is an adapter that controls the flow of information to and from the laptop when the machine is connected by using an Ethernet cable. It's called a *card* because its earliest versions in desktop PCs were plugged into the bus. When laptops arrived, they often used a plug-in NIC that installed in a PC Card slot; today nearly all computers of all types have the circuitry built into the motherboard.

- ✔ A *WiFi adapter,* which is a transmitter/receiver for wireless communication with a base station. Nearly all current laptops have a WiFi module installed in a special pocket in the base of the machine; you can easily upgrade an older machine to add wireless facilities by plugging an adapter into an ExpressCard slot or adding a device that attaches to a USB port.

# Being a Workgroup (ie)

The most common and simplest form of network, almost universally used in small offices and homes, is called *peer-to-peer.* The news you need to know here is that each of the laptops and desktop computers in this network type is considered equal; no central computer is in charge and any computer can communicate directly with another.

The essential organizing structure of a peer-to-peer network is the creation of a *workgroup* of computers. You can have more than one workgroup among computers that are physically connected to a network, although for small operations this unnecessarily complicates things.

## Creating a workgroup

The key step in creating a workgroup is electronically labeling each participating computer to Windows under the *same* identifier. The method is similar — but different — under both Windows Vista and Windows XP.

For Windows Vista users, here's the drill:

1. Click the Start button.

2. Right-click the Computer icon and choose Properties.

   The System window appears, showing the current computer name and (if one hasn't been already chosen) the default Workgroup name WORKGROUP.

3. Click either of these links:

   • Change Settings (in the Computer Name, Domain, and Workgroup section)

   • Advanced System Settings (in the menu pane on the left)

   The System Properties window appears.

4. Click the Computer Name Tab if it isn't already selected.

5. Click Change.

6. On the Computer Name Changes window you can enter a new name for your computer (or change the existing one). You can do the same for Workgroup.

   Your computer name must be unique amongst the machines on your network. It also must be fewer than 15 characters, and shouldn't include any spaces or these characters [ ] < > { } / ? # ~ ` " ' , ; : @ & ^ % | ( ) = + [ ] { }

7. Click OK to close the window.

   You're prompted to restart your computer to have the changes take effect. Once the laptop is up and running again, you can return to the System Properties window to make sure the computer and the workgroup are set up properly.

For Windows XP users, here's how:

1. Go to the Control Panel.

2. Click the System icon.

3. In the System dialog box, click the Computer Name tab.

4. Click the Change button.

5. In the Computer Name Changes dialog box, locate the Member Of pane and choose Workgroup.

6. Type in the workgroup name.

   You must exactly match the name of the workgroup on each machine. The name doesn't need to be complex or long, but should have some meaning to help you recognize it. See the preceding Remember paragraph for more restrictions.

7. Click OK twice.

## Viewing workgroup members

To see the computers that belong to a particular workgroup, follow these steps for Windows Vista machines:

1. Click the Windows button.

2. Click Network.

3. Click the down arrow alongside the Workgroup category in the window.

For Windows XP machines, do the following:

1. Click Start.

2. Click My Network Places.

3. From the left pane, choose View Workgroup Computers.

The display shows any workgroup member that's turned on and connected to the network; no offline or turned off machine is listed.

Press the ↑ key to view all workgroups that are registered on the network.

# Easing into Ethernet

Start with the physical. Here's what you need for a wired connection:

✔ A NIC. Laptop network interfaces present an RJ-45 connector, which looks like a slightly oversized telephone jack.

✔ An Ethernet cable with RJ-45 plugs. The wiring — also called a *Cat-5 cable* for standard systems and *Cat-6 cable* for the latest high-speed networks (theoretically capable of transfers as fast as 1Gbps) — attaches to the laptop NIC at one end.

✔ The other end of the Ethernet cable plugs into a router, switch, hub, or (in some arrangements) directly to another laptop or PC.

And then you come to the software side of life. Windows has come a long way from the time when early users had to configure a few dozen settings by hand. Today you can do almost all of the work using the Network Setup Wizard that's part of both Windows Vista and Windows XP. (Less capable wizards were part of the installation process for Windows ME and Windows 98 SE.) See Figure 8-1.

Here's how to use the wizard under Windows Vista or XP:

1. Make sure any network hardware is installed, turned on, and working properly on all computers in the network.

2. If you're running a version of Windows that differentiates between users and administrators, log on as an administrator.

   On nearly all laptops, the operating system is set up so the primary user is also the administrator.

3. Do one of the following:

   - Windows Vista users: Go to the Control Panel, click the Network and Sharing Center, and choose Set Up a Connection or Network.

   - Windows XP users: Choose the Start menu, click the My Network Places icon, and choose Set Up a Home or Small Office Network.

4. Answer the questions posed by the Network Setup Wizard, clicking Next after each selection.

**Figure 8-1**

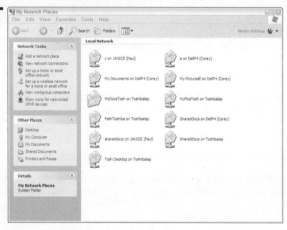

## Sharing a folder

To make a folder on a laptop available to other authorized computers in the same *local area network (LAN)*, it needs to be shared.

Here are the steps for Windows Vista users:

1. Locate and click a folder within Computer or any other Windows Explorer display (including Documents, Music, and Pictures).

2. Right-click and choose Share.

3. Fill in the form to list other persons with a user account and password for the computer you are working from. To add more users, click the link that takes you to the Network and Sharing Center.

4. You can also share the folder with other users of the current computer with or without making it available on the Internet.

   The folder can't be shared if it's marked Private in the Local Sharing and Security pane on the same dialog box.

You can enter a share name in the open entry box. A *share name* appears on-screen for other network users. You can use this to make the folder name more descriptive of its contents for others.

5. If you choose, select the Allow Network Users to Change My Files checkbox.

Stop and think before permitting others to alter your files. It's one thing to let others retrieve information from your computer, but something completely different to let them change your data or settings. On the other hand, if you're setting up a network for your own benefit — for example, preparing your laptop and desktop to exchange files for your road warrior travels — you probably want to enable this facility.

6. Click OK.

Here are the steps for Windows XP users:

1. Locate and click a folder within My Computer or any other Windows Explorer display (including My Documents, My Music, and My Pictures).

2. Right-click and choose Sharing and Security.

3. Select the Share This Folder on the Network check box.

   Click an existing check mark to remove sharing permission. The checkbox is in the Network Sharing and Security section on the Sharing tab.

4. Follow Steps 4-6 of the Vista directions.

A shared folder's icon changes to show an outstretched hand (in Windows XP) or an upside-down T (in Windows Vista) beneath its picture. When you share a folder, you make available all of its contents, including subfolders. Individual files can't be shared; you have to put them within a shared folder to be accessible.

In most cases, you don't want to share the *root folder* (the topmost folder of a disk drive) or any of the system folders that hold Windows and its settings. Keep this unavailable to avoid intentional or unintentional damage to your essential system files.

## Accessing a shared folder

When you turn on a network-enabled laptop and attach it to a network, Windows searches for files that have been set up as shared resources. Each is listed in the Local Network pane of My Network Places.

You can find the list of shared folders and access them by opening Network from the Start menu (Windows Vista) or My Network Places (Windows XP) from the desktop. Every Windows Explorer screen (as well as every Open File, Save, or Save As dialog box of applications) has a shortcut to these same two places.

## Accessing another computer on the network

After setting up your computer's networking facilities, you can see any *shared folders* offered by network computers. In Windows Vista you can also directly access a computer that's set up to share its resources:

1. From the Windows Vista desktop, click the Network icon.

2. All workgroup computers are shown. You can click View Workgroup Computers to refresh the screen if needed.

3. Double-click the icon for a listed computer and view a list of shared resources on that machine.

For Windows XP users:

1. From the Windows desktop, click the My Network Places icon.

2. Click View Workgroup Computers.

3. Double-click the icon for a listed computer and view a list of shared resources on that machine.

## Mapping a folder

You can instruct Windows to *map* a shared folder on another computer to a virtual disk drive letter on your own machine. When you perform any Open or Save command on your laptop, the shared folder appears, as if it's in your machine. The mapped folder also appears in Computer (Windows Vista) or My Computer (Windows XP).

Folders have to be already listed as shared before you can map them and you must have correct permissions to connect to them; the system administrator can set restrictions. See Figure 8-2.

To map a folder under Windows Vista, do this:

1. Click Start⇨Computer.

2. Choose Map Network Drive.

3. In the Drive list, click a drive letter.

4. Type the path to the folder or computer in the Folder box.

   Or you can click the Browse button and go to it.

5. Select the Reconnect at Logon check box.

   This make assignment permanent. To undo that setting, click to remove the check mark from the box.

6. Click Finish.

**Figure 8-2**

The process to map a folder under Windows XP and the screens are very similar. Here's how to make your map:

1. Open any Windows Explorer window, including My Network Places, My Computer, My Documents, My Music, and My Pictures.

2. Choose Tools⇨Map Network Drive.

3. From the Map Network Drive dialog box, choose a drive letter from the drop-down list.

   You can use any unassigned letter, but you might want to choose an unusual letter to help remind you of the drive's contents and location.

4. Click the Browse button and locate a shared folder on the network.

   You can choose a folder or any subfolder contained within it.

5. Select the folder or subfolder to bring up the folder's network name in the Folder box.

6. Select the Reconnect at Logon checkbox.

7. Click Finish to map the disk.

The shared folder or disk drive window appears onscreen at the end of the mapping process; you can close it.

Note that some firewall software or hardware may, by default, block access to shared folders. Consult the instructions for the device or utility to find how to allow access amongst computers on the network while protecting against intruders.

## Unmapping a folder

To remove the mapping of a network drive under Windows Vista, do the following:

1. Click Start⇨Computer.

2. Choose Tools⇨Disconnect Network Drive.

   If the Tools menu isn't displayed, press the Alt key on the keyboard once.

3. Click a drive letter in the Drive list.

4. Click OK.

You can also right-click the network drive icon in the device list, and click Disconnect.

To unmap a folder under Windows XP, do this:

1. Open any Windows Explorer window, including My Network Places, My Computer, My Documents, My Music, and My Pictures.

2. Choose Tools⇨Disconnect Network Drive.

3. Click the icon for the mapped drive you want to disconnect.

4. Click OK.

# Getting a Network Name and Address

In a nutshell, a network (including a wired or wireless Ethernet and the Internet) works by assigning a unique name or number to the sender and receiver and then wrapping that information in the small *packets* of data it sends out to the world. The recipient looks for packets with its address, snags them from the passing stream, and then reassembles the pieces into a complete file.

Every laptop connected to a network has the following identifiers:

- An *Internet protocol (IP)* address that can be established for the current session or applied permanently to a network setup.

- A MAC or physical address that's permanently encoded in the NIC installed in a machine.

- The computer's network "name."

Laptops and desktops may also make available additional information, including the computer's description ("Janice's Laptop" or "Excelsior," for example) and the list of shared resources on the computer or attached to it.

## Naming your computer

Naming a laptop or desktop computer is more than just cuteness. (One bank of machines in my office are called John, Paul, George, Ringo, Moe, Larry, and Curly. The next one up is due to be called Shemp.)

The name's important because it bridges the computer (which "thinks" only in terms of numbers) and its human users (who relate much more comfortably to names and descriptive words). A computer can very easily figure out that Janice's computer is called 192.185.1.232, but I find it a lot easier to think of the resources on her computer as residing on Paul.

You can discover your laptop's name and other information, and make changes, this way:

1.  Go to the Control Panel.

2.  Click the System icon.

3.  Under Windows Vista, consult the Computer Name, Domain, and Workgroup settings.

    Under Windows XP, choose the Computer Name tab.

4.  Under Windows Vista, click Change Settings to add a name or change the one listed.

    Under Windows XP, you can directly add or change the computer description by entering text in the on-screen box.

Your computer doesn't have to have a description; adding one is a way to help you remember some of the characteristics of differing machines you may use or that exist on the network.

5.  Click the Change button to edit the full computer name or the Workgroup name.

Each computer name on a network must be unique, and the name can have no spaces. See Figure 8-3.

Be careful with any change you make to the workgroup name. For two or more computers to share resources in a LAN, they need to be in the same workgroup and that title must be entered identically on each.

**Figure 8-3**

## Getting your laptop's IP address

Every computer that's part of a network is assigned its own ID number, known as an *IP address.* You don't need to memorize or post the number on the wall, but if you run into problems with your machine, you may be asked to provide the IP address to a technician for troubleshooting. You may also need to know the IP address when you install and configure certain external devices for the network, such as firewalls or broadband modems.

Under Windows Vista, you can discover a successfully networked computer's IP address this way:

*1.* From the Start menu, right-click Network⇨Properties.

Or, choose Start⇨Control Panel⇨Network and Internet⇨Network and Sharing Center.

*2.* Locate Connections and click View Status.

*3.* Click Details.

The computer's IP address is shown in the Value column, next to IPV4 IP Address. See Figure 8-4.

**Figure 8-4**

Under Windows XP, you can discover a successfully networked computer's IP address this way:

1. From the Windows desktop, click the My Network Places icon.

2. Locate View Network Connections and double-click your network connection.

   Your laptop may include several connections, including a wireless network, a 1394 or FireWire connection, and a LAN.

3. View the Local Area Connection Status on the General tab.

   See the connection status, the amount of time *(duration)* it's been active, and the current speed.

To understand even more technical details about your system's network configuration, you need to burrow down one or two more levels.

Under Windows XP, click the Support tab to learn the IP address, the subnet mask, and default gateway. Most users have no need to understand the gruesome details, but you may need them during troubleshooting or advanced device configuration.

One more significant detail may be of importance to a support technician. It's called the MAC address. The *media access control (MAC)* address is a unique, permanent identification assigned to each piece of hardware that's part of a network setup.

To find the MAC address, follow the preceding instructions and then click the Details button. Windows displays Network Connection Details. On this display, the MAC address is (just to confuse you) called the *physical address.*

Windows Vista users can see more information about the networking configuration on one screen. Just follow the earlier directions to display the connection properties and then click the Details button.

# Sharing Devices and Internet Connections

With a few carefully considered mouse clicks, you can make many attached components — including printers, fax devices, and broadband modems — attached to network routers or other similar hardware.

There's a great deal of value and utility in that statement. Why in the world should you have to equip each computer in an office or home with its own printer? And once you have a high-speed broadband Internet stream coming in over cable or DSL, why shouldn't you be able to share that portal with several machines at once?

## Sharing a printer

You can share a printer on a network two ways:

- ✔ Purchasing a printer that includes a built-in wired or wireless Ethernet port
- ✔ Attaching a printer to a computer and making it a shared resource

A printer with its own Ethernet interface attaches to your network hub or router and can receive instructions and data from any computer on the network; the interface can be wired or wireless. As long as the printer and the router are powered, any laptop or desktop computer can sign on to the network and use it.

If you attach a printer directly to a computer (in most situations using a USB or parallel cable), you can make that printer available to other computers on the network *anytime the computer is turned on, Windows is running, and the printer is on.*

Here's how to enable the printer for sharing under Windows Vista or Windows XP:

1. Go to the Control Panel on the computer with an attached printer.

2. Click the Printers link (Windows Vista) or the Printers and Faxes icon (Windows XP).

3. Click the printer you want to share.

4. Do one of the following:

   • Right-click and choose Sharing from the pop-up menu.

   • Choose File⇨Sharing. (Under Windows Vista, if the toolbar isn't displayed, press and release the Alt key.)

5. Click the Share This Printer checkbox, or remove the checkmark to disable the function.

   You can name the printer anything that makes sense to you; identifying its name and characteristics or its location, for example.

6. Click OK.

A shared printer's icon in XP shows an outstretched hand beneath its picture; in Vista, the icon sports the green T-bar.

## Sharing an Internet connection

You can share a broadband Internet connection two ways: one involves hardware and the other software.

For superior performance and ease of use, purchase a router that sits between the cable or DSL modem and the computers on your network. (The router hardware can connect to the computers by Ethernet cabling or wirelessly; in function it acts the same.)

One of several significant advantages to a router is that it doesn't require a particular computer to be turned on and active for another machine to access the Internet. Another strong point is that routers actively manage simultaneous requests from multiple machines.

Each network computer can access the Internet through the broadband modem simultaneously. As long as the modem and router are on, any machine that signs on to the network can use them. (A broadband modem can be shared by several machines at the same time because most users spend their time studying a web page; only a portion of the time is spent downloading information and even less time is devoted to uploading requests. The main exception: Streaming audio or video can occupy a large portion of the incoming stream.)

A less-flexible solution involves sharing a particular computer's Internet connection using Windows facilities. Here's how to enable this software solution:

1. Go to the Control Panel.

2. Under Windows Vista, click the Network and Sharing Center.

   Under Windows XP, click the Network Connections icon.

3. Click an Internet connection, a modem, or an *Internet service provider (ISP)* icon.

4. Do one of the following:

   • Right-click and choose Properties.

   • Choose File⇨Properties. (If the toolbar isn't displayed in Windows Vista, press and release the Alt key.)

5. From the Properties dialog box, click the Advanced tab.

6. Select the Allow Other Network Users to Connect Through This Computer's Internet Connection checkbox to enable sharing, or deselect to disable sharing.

7. Click OK.

Under this scheme, any computer on the network can locate an Internet connection through its Network Connections window.

---

## Wirelessly Networking

I've already noted that in many ways, connecting to a wireless network is very much like connecting to a wired one . . . without the wires. Operations within your laptop are the same, but instead of going to a wired *transmitter/receiver (transceiver)* called a NIC, your system communicates with a wireless transceiver.

The signal proceeds through space (typically no more than a few hundred feet in ideal conditions) and then it's picked up by a wireless transceiver that can be within another laptop, attached to a desktop machine, or is part of a device called a *router,* which spreads the signal of a network to multiple points. See Figure 8-5.

Broadband cable modem or DSL phone modem      WiFi-equipped laptop

**Figure 8-5**

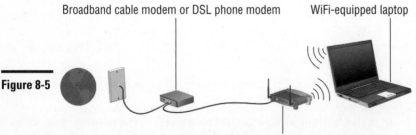

Wireless router communicates with wireless devices and connects to wired Ethernet

Courtesy of Hewlett-Packard Company

The beauty of modern laptops, in combination with Windows Vista or Windows XP, is that they come well set up to use standard devices and preset radio frequencies to communicate with almost any system within range. As a user, you're required to do the following:

  ✔ Enable Windows to use the WiFi adapter. If you've purchased a machine with all equipment present, this should already be accomplished.

  ✔ Turn on the adapter. Most wireless systems have a small switch that must be enabled to send power to the adapter; in addition to saving power when the WiFi circuitry isn't in use, this lets you block signals in certain places where they may not be allowed, such as within airplanes and certain high-security locations.

  ✔ Meet the sign-on requirements of whatever system you want to communicate with.

That last assignment used to be the rub, the place where high-tech ran into mere-mortal users. Today, though, many public access systems and subscription services do all the work for you; all you need to do is turn on your laptop, turn on your WiFi hardware, and load your Internet browser.

You see a sign-on screen that may only ask for your name, or you may have to sign up and receive a password. And if the service charges for its use, enter a credit card number or other means of payment; some services run by cell phone operators add the charges to your already established account.

On the other hand, if you're linking up to a private network — including one you set up in your own office or home, or if you're given access to a network that doesn't have an automatic sign-on — you may have to use one of the utilities offered within Windows.

Windows Vista users can automate most of the process by clicking Start⇨Network. From the Network window, click the button helpfully labeled Add a Wireless Device to the Network.

On a laptop running Windows XP, you can get to the Wireless Network Setup Wizard through the Control Panel. If you're using the Classic view, click Wireless Network Setup Wizard. If you're using the Category view of the Control panel, click Network and Internet Connections⇨Wireless Network Setup Wizard. See Figure 8-6.

The elements of a manually established connection include the following:

  ✔ Network name (also known as *SSID*). The *Service Set Identifier* — an acronym that's never used — is the name given to the network; that ID is converted into a 32-character code that is part of the header for every packet sent over the wireless network.

✔ Network key. You can have Windows automatically assign a 26-digit hexa-decimal key to lock away unauthorized users, or you can manually assign the key. There's no reason not to use the automatic assignment for the first device set up; after that you can manually enter it on other devices, use a flash memory key to transfer it, or use an automated setup program sup-plied by your router or other network hardware maker.

✔ WPA encryption. You can instruct the system to use the safer *WiFi Protected Access (WPA)* instead of the standard *Wireless Encryption Protocol (WEP)* standard; not all devices can use WPA, so make sure all the devices are com-patible. If WPA doesn't work, fall back to WEP. If you're connecting at a public hotspot, the operator may insist that these encryption schemes be turned off and the company's own proprietary system used.

**Figure 8-6**

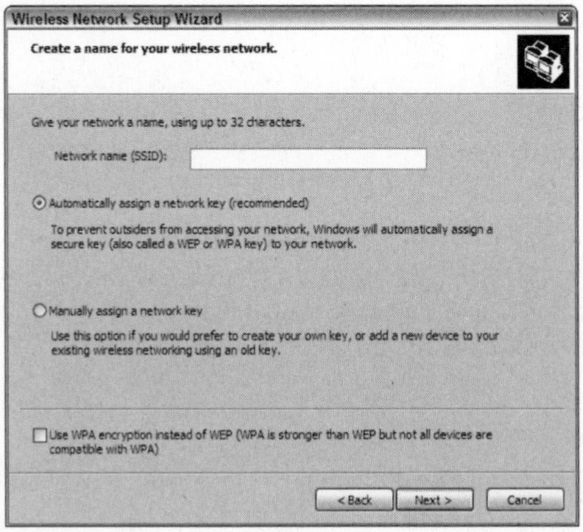

All this work may be unnecessary if you purchase a router to set up your own wireless network; that device may come with software that loads on your laptop and on each of the other devices you authorize to use the network.

# The Internet

Computers are wondrous devices, but when you think about it, the technology that's probably changed your life more than anything else is the Internet. In just a decade or so it has become the thread that links just about everyone together wherever they are and however they travel. My laptop and I live on the Internet. Assignments come in by e-mail, there's little I can't find out a few clicks into a Google session, and the work goes out over the web. And then the dollars go out to the bank and shopping web sites; my wallet gets very little exercise.

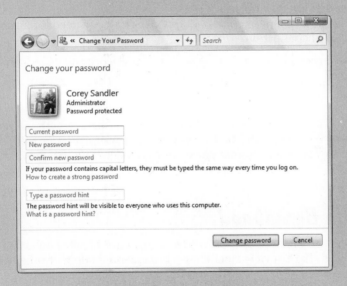

## In this part . . .

- ✔ **Going online**
- ✔ **Connecting different ways**

# Connecting to the Internet

Although a laptop can connect to the Internet many ways, in the current world of high-speed, broadband communication these two methods are most often employed:

- Hitching a ride through a router (wired or wireless) to a broadband modem connected to a shared cable from a cable television provider, a fiber-optics cable, a *digital subscriber line (DSL),* or a specialized Internet pipeline.

- In a pinch, using a dial-up modem and *plain old telephone service (POTS)* to call an *Internet service provider (ISP)* for a relatively slow, unshared link.

Some users, located in corners of the world beyond the reach of cable or DSL service, use satellite downlinks for Internet connection. The good news is that nearly every current laptop comes equipped with all you need for any of these various types of connection:

- An Ethernet adapter for wired access to a network and its modem

- A WiFi adapter, to communicate with a wireless router for the same sort of access, and a dial-up modem

If your laptop lacks any of these facilities, you can add them with the purchase of an adapter that plugs into the ExpressCard slot (or the PC Card slot on an older machine) or as an external device that connects to a USB port.

# Connecting via Broadband

A laptop that's configured to work with a *local area network (LAN)* is all set to share files and share devices, including a broadband modem or other high-speed Internet connection. It's literally a matter of plugging and playing. You may, though, need permission from the network administrator of a system other than your own to gain access to shared devices like a broadband modem and network content.

The Internet is all around: in wireless signals, as part of shared access on a wired network, in direct connection from your laptop to a high-speed broadband cable, fiber-optic cable, or DSL modem, and at the other end of a telephone wire.

When you consider Internet connections, you usually think in terms of download speeds, which is for most users the most important (but not the only) element of the service. In most Internet connections, the capacity is split in a way that devotes a larger portion of the signal to *downloading* — displaying web pages, receiving e-mail, and streaming audio and video — than it does to uploading. The fact is that most users require only a smaller (and slower) channel to request that material be sent.

In any case, computing faster is almost always better and that's certainly true when it comes to surfing on the World Wide Web. The fastest Internet download speeds for most laptop users are shown in order here.

| *Connection* | *Download Speed* | *Description* |
|---|---|---|
| T-carrier | 1,544 to 44,736 kbps | The backbones for many types of wired telecommunication are T1 and T3 services. Connecting a single laptop to a T3 *backbone* to the Internet is sort of like hooking up your garden hose to the exit pipe of the Hoover Dam. T3 connections serve huge businesses or government agencies, or college campuses. The older, slower T1 connection was at one time the fastest pipe. |
| Fiber optics | 5,000 to 20,000 kpbs, and climbing | Fiber optic providers, including industry-leader Verizon with its FIOS service, are beginning to make inroads in parts of the country. Verizon has introduced its service in densely populated urban areas. The fiber cable (like cable television service) is "unbalanced," meaning that the download speed is much faster than the upload; this matches the way most users employ the connection. Typical offerings include 5 mbps download and 2 mbps upload, 15 mbps/2 mbps, 20 mbps/5 mbps, and in some markets 30 mbps/5 mbps. The fiber cable can also be used to bring telephone and video service. |
| Cable | 1,500 to 10,000 kbps, and climbing | Cable TV providers have used unused frequencies on the relatively thick and fast coaxial or fiber optic cable that also carries reruns of *I Love Lucy* and the latest vapid reality television show. The theoretical top speed for cable can be reduced if many heavy users are between your home or office and the cable company's "head end"; however, new technologies are pushing more bits down the cable and some companies are offering even faster connections for a little more. In my office, I typically receive downloads at speeds of about 7,188 kbps (7.1 mbps), while files or commands I send travel at about 2,100 kbps (2.1 mbps) — still much faster than almost any available alternative for an individual or small business. |

cont.

| Connection | Download Speed | Description |
|---|---|---|
| DSL | 512 to 3,000 kbps | DSL employs unused frequencies on POTS wires. As with cable, the actual speed can be reduced if many other heavy-duty users are between your modem and the central office; DSL can also be affected by the quality of old wiring and switching equipment. In some markets, phone companies have managed to squeeze even more speed out of certain wires, with theoretical download speeds as high as 24,000 kbps. |
| Satellite | 700 to 1,000 kbps | Downloads from a satellite are generally an acceptable compromise for users who are too remote from a wired high-speed connection; requests for data and uploads are sent over a conventional phone line or by a slower satellite uplink. |
| ISDN | 256 to 1,000 kbps | Another POTS-based system, it's been mostly replaced by DSL. |
| Dial-up | Up to 53 kbps | The top speed from this, otherwise known as a 56K modem, is capped by technical and regulatory limits, and may be reduced by the quality of phone wiring, switches, and other local equipment. |

# Wireless Internet Options

To make a WiFi connection, you'll find one of four situations, each with different requirements:

- ✔ **A true public access wireless network.** Some coffee shops, fast food restaurants, cafes, hotels, public libraries, schools, and community organizations offer this kind. You may be asked to sign in, but there's no subscription fee. In most cases the login page gives the necessary information for any settings you may have to make for your wireless hardware and software.

- ✔ **An unsecured private wireless network.** You may find that a neighbor has a wireless router in his home that hasn't been secured against outsiders, or a similar situation in an office or public space. You're making use of someone else's signal and subscription to an Internet provider, but on the other hand, the owner hasn't bothered to take the simple steps necessary to shut you out. The signal owner may or may not intend to share it with strangers; as far as I'm concerned, this is about the same as someone complaining that you are listening to his stereo on the beach. The operator of a wireless network should either make it private or leave it open. If left open, he or she should accept the possibility that passersby will hitchhike on the airwaves.

✔ **A short-term pay-as-you-go service.** You'll find companies selling hourly, daily, or weekly access in airports, hotels, and resorts. When you reach the login page, you'll likely be asked to provide a credit card number.

✔ **A subscription service with access across a city, a region, or the entire country.** Cell phone companies, ISPs, and other businesses offer this kind. Examples include the following:

- T-Mobile's HotSpot service with thousands of wireless hubs in coffee shops, business centers, and hotels.

- Verizon Wireless Broadband Access service, which claims coverage in some 250 metropolitan areas and more than 230 primary airports in the United States, using a system that's an offshoot of cell phone service.

You may be able to sign up for the service anywhere you find it, but generally you have to enable an account before you travel.

# Connecting via Dial-up Modem

On the one hand, using a dial-up modem is relatively simple because you can set up access from home or office and then carry it with you. And you'll find standard telephone service almost everywhere in the United States and Canada; connections in other foreign countries can sometimes require a bit of extra effort.

The not-so-good news, as I've already noted, is that dial-up modem communication has been left in the dust by much faster broadband systems; the cable modem in my office generally delivers downloads at about 7,200 kilobytes per second (kbps), which is something on the order of 140 times faster than the best you can hope for from a 56K modem.

However, broadband still hasn't reached some places. Today, most people consider their laptop's built-in modem an emergency tool; in the past few years, I've used the modem exactly once (when I found myself working in the far edge of the distant reaches of the most remote boondocks — up the bayou in Louisiana, to be precise), but I was certainly glad it was there.

If you haven't set up your dial-up modem, you may find it easiest to enlist the assistance of the help desk at your ISP; some national providers offer CDs that automatically make settings and install phone numbers.

To do it yourself, you need to know the following information:

 ✔ At least one telephone number for telecommunications with your ISP. This is different from the support number. It's also helpful to obtain local phone numbers for the places you travel to eliminate long distance charges.

✔ The *username* for your account.

✔ The *password* for your account.

With that information in hand, you can use the Windows New Connection Wizard. Here is some general advice for the process.

For Windows Vista users:

1. Click Start⇨Control Panel⇨Network and Internet⇨Network and Sharing Center⇨Manage Network Connections.

2. Follow the onscreen instructions to identify authorized users of the new connection.

3. Select the means for connecting (dial-up or through the Internet).

4. Follow the general Steps 4 through 8 listed for Windows XP, which follow.

For Windows XP users:

1. Choose Start⇨All Programs⇨Accessories ⇨Communications ⇨ New Connection Wizard.

2. Click Next⇨Connect to the Internet⇨Next.

3. Click Set Up My Connection Manually⇨Next⇨Connect Using a Dial-up Modem⇨Next.

4. Enter a name for the service you'll use and click Next.

   The name can be your ISP's name or a nickname.

5. Enter the phone number for data communication with your ISP.

   Later you can change the phone number or add necessary details like 9 (dialing 9 and pausing for an outside line, as required in some offices or hotels) or 1 plus an area code.

6. Enter the username for your established account with the ISP.

7. Enter the account password in the text box and again in the Confirm Password text box.

8. Click Next⇨Finish.

## Making a dial-up connection

Other than speed, the biggest difference between broadband and dial-up is the fact that with dial-up, you need to initiate a session — like placing a phone call — and you need to hang up when you're done.

Follow the necessary steps:

1. Make sure your modem is properly installed in the laptop, inserted in the ExpressCard or PC Card slot, or connected to a USB port.

   You can check the status by going to the Control Panel and clicking System⇨Hardware tab⇨Device Manager, and then expand the Modem category by clicking the +. The properties screen tells you if the device is functioning properly and has the appropriate drivers installed.

2. Ensure there is a telephone cable connected between the laptop modem and a phone wall outlet.

   If you have any doubts about whether the outlet is active, plug a telephone into the outlet and check for a dial tone.

3. Click a program that requires an Internet connection.

   Programs include a web browser such as Internet Explorer or a proprietary communications service such as AOL. If these programs are properly configured, they automatically begin dialing out on the modem. (If you alternate between the dial-up modem and other connections such as WiFi or wired Ethernet, the program may ask you to choose one of these modes.)

4. When you're through with your dial-up session, disconnect from the phone line.

   Some programs offer a button that does this for you; you can do so manually by right-clicking the modem icon in the system tray's notification area and choosing Disconnect. A less elegant way to disconnect is to unplug the telephone cable from the wall or the laptop.

A few warnings about dial-up modem use:

✔ Never plug your modem into an office or hotel system without first checking with a knowledgeable technician or manager to see if the system uses standard analog telephone components (that's what you want) or digital technology. Digital phone systems may carry higher voltage levels than your laptop modem is expecting, and can damage both the modem and your computer.

✔ Run the phone cable along the wall or otherwise out of the way to prevent a tangled-foot accident that could damage your laptop (or you).

✔ If you're using a hotel's phone system, never assume that local or toll-free calls are free of charge. If local calls are free but the number for your ISP is out of the area, configure your modem's dial-up properties to use a prepaid or billable phone card, which is almost always significantly less expensive than the rates charged by hotels.

## Creating dialing rules

The whole idea of a laptop is that you can lug it from place to place, and if you're going to use a dial-up modem as your emergency communication, you'll find it much more convenient if you automate the rules of engagement as much as possible.

The key here is to create as many "locations" as you need for the various places you may use the modem. Each location includes a local phone number plus rules that instruct the machine on how to reach an outside line and dial. (In some places, for example, you may need to dial 9 for an outside line; in others, you may need to add 1+*area code* to reach even a local number.)

In Vista, choose Hardware and Sound⇨Phone and Modem Options to get to the modem settings. Here's how to set up a location in both Classic Windows Vista view and in Windows XP:

1. On the Control Panel, double-click the Phone and Modem Options icon.

2. If not already selected, click the Dialing Rules tab.

   • If you've previously set up locations, they're listed; you can choose to edit any of them.

   • If you haven't yet set up a location, Windows displays a "New Location" for you to work with. The operating system assumes that this location is in the area code you provided when you first installed or configured Windows. Click Edit to set up the location.

3. Enter a location name for the first defined place.

   Be as specific as you can, including a particular place like your Main Office, or the Peoria Field Office, or the name of a client or hotel you know you'll use.

4. Enter the location's country/region and the area code.

5. Carefully work your way through the dialing rules.

   Dialing rules are listed in the following table. If you're uncertain about any of the details, you may have to experiment when you and your laptop are at the location you're defining.

   Leave the appropriate line blank if the location doesn't require special codes for local or long-distance calls.

6. The location assumes that the phone line you're using employs tone dialing; if your location hangs on to old-fashioned pulse dialing, change the indicator from Tone to Pulse.

7. Click the Area Code Rules tab to set dialing instructions within the specified area code.

   - Click Edit to amend an existing rule.

   - Click New to create an entry.

   On this tab you can instruct the modem to dial one of these ways:

   - 1 + area code

   - Area code

   - 1

   - Another digit for all prefixes

   - Another digit for those indicated

8. If using a prepaid or billable phone account, click the Calling Card tab.

9. Enter information, including the access number and your PIN.

If entering your access number and PIN make you a bit nervous about the security of such information, that's good; make sure your Windows operating system is password protected and be sure to notify the phone company if the laptop goes missing.

| Option | Dialing Rule |
|--------|--------------|
| To access an outside line for local calls | Insert the necessary code, often a 9 or 8 to get an outside line. You may need to add one or more commas to force a short pause in the dialing sequence for use with certain systems. |
| To access an outside line for local calls | Insert the necessary code, often a 9 or 8 followed by a 1 to get an outside line for a long-distance call. Some systems may require entry of a user code to allow departmental billing. |
| Use this carrier code to make long-distance calls | Some users place long-distance calls through a dial-up phone portal, which requires entry of an access code before the number to be dialed. |
| Use this carrier code to make international calls | Similar to the long-distance carrier code, this is an access code for calls out of the country. |
| To disable call waiting | Click the checkbox, then enter the code that prevents call waiting tones from interfering with a dial-up connection. For example, some systems shut off call waiting for the current call with *70. |
| Tone versus pulse code | If you've still got a phone line with a pulse code, you may need to update facilities; are you sure you have an electric power line, too? |

# Road Tips

Your computer's safest when it's at home: It's less likely to be stolen, lost, dropped, or intruded upon. On the other hand, this book is about laptops, and these marvelous machines are intended to be on the move. They (and their owners) go through airports, hotels, Internet cafes, and places in between. And threats are everywhere: people who want to steal your hardware, steal the information on your machine, or steal your good name.

## In this part . . .

- ✔ Employing best practices for moving laptops
- ✔ Using security and system maintenance utilities

# Be Careful Out There

The good news about using computers is that you can keep so many of the details of your life in one relatively compact place, and you can manage your affairs remotely: You can bank, pay bills, make investments, buy and sell items, and communicate all sorts of personal information.

The bad news is that bad people out there are constantly looking for ways to steal from you.

As a laptop user, you have three serious exposures to thieves:

✔ Someone could steal your portable computer and with it all the information contained within.

✔ Someone could conduct an electronic break-in to the data stored on your computer by sneaking in through an unguarded port to the Internet.

✔ Someone could intercept information you transmit over a wired or wireless network or the Internet and use it to your detriment with banks, employers, or *Entertainment Tonight*.

In this section I deal with each of these threats in detail. But let me start with this three-part plan: Read this chapter carefully, follow the instructions as closely as you can for your particular situation, and make it a point to reassess your personal security procedures every few months.

I begin with some general thoughts about best practices to protect your laptop and its contents as you travel. Then I discuss ways to physically lock your laptop to make it more difficult to pilfer. And finally, I deal with ways to make the contents of your hard drive unavailable to a thief.

# Copping Best Practices for Laptops On the Move

Most people are pretty well acquainted with the facts of life on the road: You limit the amount of cash you carry, you avoid flashing around large bills, and you keep your wallet deeply buried. That's all good.

Now consider this: When you walk around town, an airport, or a hotel with a rectangular, reinforced cloth or leather briefcase slung over your shoulder, you might as well be carrying a flashing neon sign that reads, "I'm carrying a $1,500 laptop computer that's yours if you can snatch it. And if you're quick and smart — and if I haven't properly protected my personal information on the disk drive — you can get into my bank and credit card accounts before I notify the financial institutions of the theft."

And believe it or not, nearly everyone has, at one time or another, accidentally left the computer bag behind at a check-in counter, at a restaurant, in a waiting room, or in an overhead or under-seat storage space on an airplane. It only takes a few seconds for a quick grab to lead to a prolonged headache.

The first step you should take is to consider how you treat your laptop's physical security. Here are some suggestions:

- ✓ Make sure you have a sturdy bag to hold your computer.

- ✓ Remove logos or buy a more nondescript bag. My first few laptop cases came festooned with the logo of the computer manufacturer. Why in the world would you want to make the expensive contents of your bag even more obvious?

- ✓ Just in case you misplace your computer and it is found by an honest person, make sure your bag has more than a few tags with your name and phone number listed; you might want to add the phrase "Reward for Return," but not your home or office address. Some users (and some companies) have decided not to list the name of their company on the contact information to make it just slightly more difficult for a thief to use information on the hard disk.

- ✓ You can subscribe to a number of services that sells stickers or tags to attach to your bag or to the laptop itself; the company lists its phone number and address and acts as an intermediary to help arrange for the return of a laptop found by a Good Samaritan, a police agency, or anyone else who happens to have it.

- ✓ Don't write down your computer and web site passwords in a notebook or on a sheet of paper and store it in your laptop case. If you absolutely must have a written record of your passwords, encrypt them (I show you a few methods later in this chapter) and put them in your wallet or in a buttoned pocket of your jacket or in the suitcase with your dirty socks.

- ✓ Don't leave your house and car keys in the laptop case. To begin with, your key ring shouldn't have your name and address on it; that way, if you lose your keys away from home, there's little chance someone will figure out who they belong to and what doors the keys open. But if you store the keys in your laptop case and there's any way for a thief to figure out your home or office address, you have undone that safeguard.

- ✓ Develop a strategy for getting through airport security (and some building X-ray machines) that allows you to keep a constant eye on your laptop. What I do is this: I put my shoes, my coat, my empty briefcase, and everything else through the scanning machine first. Then I watch to see that they go through before I walk through the metal detector. If I went through before the computer passed into the machine, I could find myself on the wrong side of a security barrier and out of sight of the laptop. An even better solution: When you travel with someone else, split up the task — one goes through the machine first and keeps track of items coming through on the belt, while the other lags behind to watch their progress.

# Hiding the Hardware

Would you notice if a delivery person walked by your cubicle with a box or sack about $10 \times 12"$ — about the size of the laptop that used to be on someone's desk down the hall? How long would it take you to realize that your laptop had been removed from its rightful place on the desk in your dorm? In your office, would the night watchman notice if a cleaning person swept a laptop into a trash bag that was headed out of the door?

The fact is that the very portability that makes a laptop so valuable to people who do their work in various places at various times also makes it very easy to steal. It's impractical to carry your machine everywhere you go . . . and some companies may not want you to take the laptop home unless it's in connection with a business trip. It may also be impractical to store a laptop in a safe or locked closet.

But here's one thing you can do to make it more difficult for a casual thief to grab your laptop from your desk at work, your desk at home, or your desk in a motel: Use a *security cable.* Almost all current laptops include a hardened slot at the back of the machine (see Figure 10-1) designed to work with special cables and locks that can attach to a desk, pipe, or other fixed object.

**Figure 10-1**

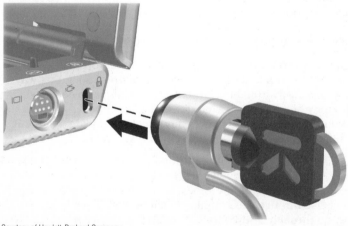

Courtesy of Hewlett-Packard Company

One example is the MicroSaver Portable Notebook Combination Lock from Kensington, which is very well summed up by its name. This small device — about the size of a desktop mouse, as shown in Figure 10-2 — includes a retractable 4'-long aircraft-grade steel cable; the end that plugs into the security slot of the laptop includes a three-tumbler combination lock. That's probably just enough to convince a snatch-and-run thief to go elsewhere.

**Figure 10-2**

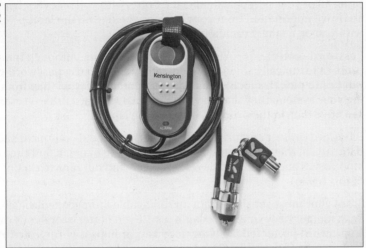

One step up in security is the MicroSaver Alarmed Computer Lock; this device uses a circular key — you get a second key to hide away, but I suggest you not lose the original while you're traveling — and also offers a loud, battery-powered alarm that sounds if someone tampers with the lock.

These devices aren't perfect — a thief could break the laptop case to free it from the lock, but that would reduce its resale value. Or he could bring a huge cable cutter; there's no defense against a thief who's truly dedicated or brazen. Instead, the devices serve the same purpose as most home burglar alarms, which also are imperfect; the idea is to convince a thief to move on to an easier target and leave your property alone.

## Locking Down Your Data

Now move on from the physical to the metaphysical: safeguarding the information stored on your machine. For many, although losing a laptop would be an expensive event, that price pales in comparison to the value of the information stored on the hard drive. You could lose your job, your security clearance, your banking and investment information, and all sorts of sensitive corporate or personal information.

These six ideas reduce the chances that a thief or a finder-and-keeper can use the information on your laptop:

✔ Be careful about what you store on your laptop. Do you really need to bring all of your personal financial records with you on every trip? Does sensitive information from your business belong on the laptop you take with you on a family vacation?

✔ Password-protect your Windows operating system. Although this isn't foolproof (a technically savvy and dedicated thief can use password-cracking utilities to pick this lock), it usually prevents the casual thief from accessing your system; they may have to reformat the hard drive — erasing your sensitive data in the process — to use the laptop.

✔ Password-protect compressed Zip folders that hold your most sensitive data. Again, these passwords aren't impossible to crack, but they usually stop casual and amateur thieves. (You can find out how to do this in Part 5 of this book.)

✔ Store your most sensitive data on removable storage media such as a flash memory key or a recordable disc. Even better, store your data on a password-protected flash memory key, or in password-protected Zip folders on a CD or DVD. Keep these forms of removable media anywhere *other* than in your laptop or its case; some flash memory keys take their name literally and attach to your keyring, which you can keep in your pocket.

✔ Never enable your web favorites to automatically log you in with your username and password. That's the equivalent of leaving the front door open and the safe unlocked. You can, though, use a password manager program that retains an encrypted record of all of your usernames and passwords and automatically fills them in; you need to unlock that single program each time you turn on your laptop or each time you load your Windows browser.

✔ For industrial-strength protection, use a hardware encryption scheme that scrambles all of your data and locks it away behind a complex password. This sort of system is almost impossible to crack.

## Hard disk encryption

Hardware encryption comes in two types: one is entirely software based and the other combines a plug-in key with software protection.

Kensington, found at www.kensington.com, is among manufacturers who offer consumer-level authentication and encryption devices. The PCKey combines an access key that plugs into the laptop's USB port with a password authentication; both the key and password are required before anyone can use the machine and any network to which it's connected.

All data on the hard drive is encrypted; when an application requests the encoded data, it passes through the PCKey filter and is decrypted to be stored in the computer's system memory for the application. All data written back to the hard drive is reencrypted.

PCKey software employs 128-bit *Advanced Encryption Standard (AES)* to encrypt data; this renders information on the drive all but impossible to read unless you're employed by the National Security Agency and have a couple hundred supercomputers and an unlimited amount of time and money . . . you get the idea: No ordinary thief is going to be able to read your disk. If you forget your password or lose the PCKey device, contact Kensington and (after answering a set of questions) regain access to your data.

An example of a software-only solution can be found in products such as those offered by GuardianEdge Technologies, at www.guardianedge.com. These products are for office environments with an administrator or IT department.

## Hiding behind a firewall

Some people erect a wall first, and then lock away their possessions. I prefer to do it the other way around; once I'm reasonably sure that all of my private data is secured within my laptop and I have a means of locking down the machine itself, I build a barricade. Call it a belt-and-suspenders safety system.

Why software first and hardware last? Because when it comes to a laptop, the software goes with you anywhere you travel, but the hardware at your destination may be different from the equipment on your desk.

When you're connecting to the Internet from your office or home, you're likely connecting through a router or other appliance that includes a hardware *firewall* intended to block unauthorized intrusions to your system. However, when you're on the road and connecting on an ad hoc basis through a wireless system, the front (and back) doors to your laptop are wide open; you're relying entirely on the good intentions of those around you (ha!) and the ability of Windows and third-party software utilities to turn away evildoers and pranksters.

A bit of explanation: A firewall isn't a physical bubble that encases your laptop; instead, it's a circuit and a bit of memory that serve as a checkpoint for anything coming in or going out of the machine. Your laptop is smart enough to electronically configure itself in a logical manner even if the pieces aren't lined up physically.

If you're connecting through a trusted network — at a client or a friend's home — you may benefit from the hardware firewall they have in place. But in any case, I suggest you also use either the built-in software firewall that's part of Windows or a third-party software program.

Microsoft offers basic software firewall and Internet security features as part of Windows XP (and an improved set of facilities in Windows Vista). The included firewall and privacy controls should be your starting point for protecting against unwanted intrusion.

For Windows Vista users, the Windows firewall (see Figure 10-3) is reachable as an icon on the Control Panel. You can turn the firewall on or off by clicking one of the commands in the menu pane on the left side of the window. You can also manually allow a particular program through the firewall.

As a Windows XP user, you can reach the Windows Security Center by going to the Control Panel and double-clicking the Security Center icon. The other half of the built-in protections for security are on the Internet Properties page; from the Control Panel, double-click the Internet Options icon.

The tabs on the properties page include a Privacy section aimed at blocking web sites from placing *cookies* that may harvest information about you without your permission. See Figure 10-4.

**Figure 10-3**

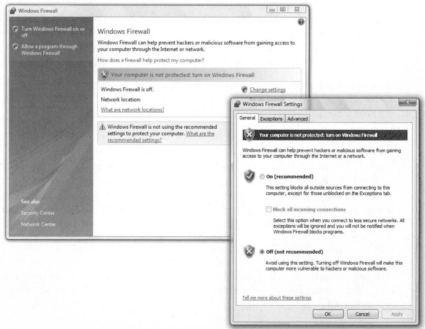

**Figure 10-4**

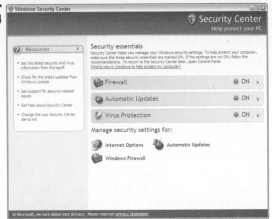

I recommend installing other software, including an antivirus program, an adware tracker, and a more robust software or hardware firewall whenever the situation permits. And many users, myself included, prefer to use more robust software firewalls including those offered by Symantec (as part of its Norton series of utilities) or McAfee's SecurityCenter.

The firewall included in Norton 360 v2.0 (see Figure 10-5) includes some features not yet offered by Symantec. The SONAR technology is designed to detect unknown malware or spyware based on unusual behavior and to automatically adjust the firewall to protect against the new threat.

**Figure 10-5**

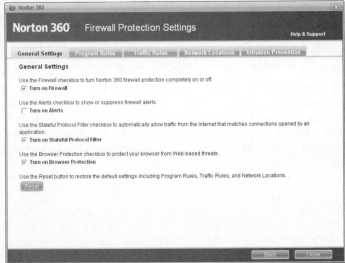

# Making a Tough Password

There are passwords, and there are 6SJ7&!@#! passwords.

Do you really think you're being clever and original by using your pet's name or the last four digits of your Social Security number or your local sports team's mascot spelled backwards? Trust me, hackers and crackers are at least as smart as you when it comes to passwords — that's where they would start.

Here's a much better password: Gess_Wh()_l607

Take that password apart.

It begins with a misspelled word that's easy to remember: *Gess* rather than *Guess*. It also includes upper- and lowercase letters. Then there's a nonalphabetic underscore. And then there's a second misspelled word, substituting *()* for the letter *o*, followed by an underscore. And finally, there's a meaningful number — in this case the year of Henry Hudson's first voyage, a meaningful date to me because I've written a book on the subject; but if you look closely you see that I substituted a lowercase *l* for the numeral *1* in the password.

Go over some of the dos and don'ts of constructing a good password:

- ✔ **Make it meaningful but obscure.** A totally random password like J8kl)$32H*/xc is a very strong defense, but it is also very difficult to remember and in some cases a password-cracking program may be able to determine the method used by your software's random-password generator.

  Don't include the name of a popular singer of today; on the other hand, if you're a fan of a long-gone crooner, that's an interesting tack. How about Jenny Lind, the "Swedish Nightingale" who made her American debut in 1850? Here's a password based on that: 18/Jenny_Lind/Nightingale/50.

- ✔ **Make it private information.** Don't use your day of birth, year of birth, your wife or husband's name, your children's names, or anything else that a determined hacker can find in public records.

- ✔ **Longer's better than shorter.** Depending on where you're using the password — as the entrance key to Windows or into a secure web site — passwords can be as short as six characters or more than 100 characters in length. I don't recommend going for something that long, but then again you might just want to use some unusual phrase, joke, or combination of words . . . with a twist.

✔ **Don't be predictable.** If you want to include the word CROONER in your password, try replacing one or both of the letters *o* with a *0*. Or even better, try something odd like a pair of parenthesis to represent the *o*. One example: cR()()ner.

✔ **Use spaces, underscores, numbers, and keyboard symbols.** In some situations, you can also use special characters accessible from the keyboard through complex combinations like Alt+234, which yields the Ω (Omega) character. The further you go away from passwords based on words in the dictionary, the better off you are.

✔ **Change your passwords every few months.** I know that is easier said than done, but it's a good practice just in case someone has picked up some of your personal information and is poised to attack. One way to avoid having to come up with a completely new password is to create a replaceable component. For example, if your current password is Jenny_Lind/Nightingale/3Q+Eggplant; then when the fourth quarter comes around you could change it to Jenny_Lind/Nightingale/4Q+Rutabaga.

✔ **Don't write down your password anywhere near your laptop or desktop.** Notice that I didn't say "don't write down your password." Although that's good advice, it isn't realistic; I don't know about your memory, but mine is pretty well maxed out. Instead, though, come up with some kind of short-hand that's obvious to you and no one else.

For example, to remember Jenny_Lind/Nightingale/3Q+Eggplant as the password for your Bank of Oshkosh account, you might write down *B'gosh Swedish Parmigiana.* B'gosh is a memory cue for Oshkosh. Swedish should remind you of Jenny Lind, the Swedish Nightingale. You know what quarter you're in, and Parmigiana should prompt you to use Eggplant. (You also have to remember, or use dummy code as a reminder, your password format, including underscores, slashes, and plus marks.)

✔ **Consider using password manager software.** Several are available as shareware from Internet sites (although that source makes me nervous for something as important as your passwords). In version 2.0, Norton 360 added an Identity Safe module that encrypts and manages usernames and passwords; it automatically fills in logins and forms for you behind a single password. Phishing protection guards online attempts to steal your personal information by verifying web sites and blocking fraudulent sites. See Figure 10-6.

**Figure 10-6**

# Managing Internet Safety

One of the beauties of traveling with a laptop is also one of its potential horrors: wireless Internet communication at public hotspots. The chances of someone eavesdropping on your exchange of data with a WiFi router is pretty slim, but not out of the realm of possibility. The best solution is to always act as if someone is listening in.

Here are some practices and solutions to consider:

✔ Make certain your antivirus software is active and updated.

✔ Turn off file and folder sharing on your laptop if you're connected to a public network; otherwise, you're leaving the back door open while you peek out the front.

✔ Don't unnecessarily conduct banking, credit card, and investment activities while on the road. If you must, carefully examine your online and printed statements for questionable transactions in the weeks and months that follow any use of your laptop on the road. Notify the banks immediately if you see something amiss.

✔ Any time you're offered a "secure" login, accept that option. (Such logins are generally standard for banking sites and also available at web-based e-mail portals and some other locations.) Although the Internet will respond slightly slower than usual, this adds a layer of encryption between your browser and its destination and back.

✔ If something seems wrong with your machine while you're connected to a WiFi network, assume that something is. Things to look for:

- Warning messages from your antivirus software

- Unusual churning of your hard disk drive when it's usually silent

- Unexpected messages from your browser or e-mail software

And so on. When in doubt, disconnect.

✔ Consider adding an anonymous surfing utility that hides your laptop behind the skirts of an intermediary computer. For example, Anonymous Surfing from Anonymizer blocks the pass-through of your *Internet protocol (IP)* address when you're on the Internet, which should prevent unscrupulous or overzealous marketers from figuring out your identity when you're online. The product also encrypts your confidential information sent out over a wireless connection.

- Anonymizer Anonymous Surfing, at www.anonymizer.com, works exactly as promised, although the fact that all of your work goes through a barricade reduces the net speed of your connection by as much as 50 percent. That may not be too high a price to pay for a road warrior far away from home.

- Other services include Proxify, at www.proxify.com, which allows you to go to any web site by first logging on to an intermediary site; the places you visit will not be able to find out your IP address, only that of the intermediary site. You subscribe for a period of time; a subscription costs about $80 per year.

✔ Free services like Behidden (www.behidden.com) and The Cloak (www.the-cloak.com) offer a limited amount of daily anonymous surfing. Both services provide more access if you purchase a subscription.

# Picking Up after Yourself

If you've ever watched *CSI*, you've seen how police forensic scientists pounce on a computer at a crime scene and within minutes come back with a full report on virtually every bit of business and online conversation for the past few weeks. Some of what they do is Hollywood hokum, but there is a kernel of truth involved: Your Internet browser does keep track of much of what you do and where you go.

I've already mentioned Anonymizer and other products and services of that sort; they work to prevent outsiders from reaching into your machine and identifying it and you. But the other half of the equation involves cleaning up the trail that your own machine makes. Do you want anyone who uses your machine to know what web sites you've visited and what images or videos have appeared on your screen from an Internet source?

Some people occasionally do a bit of online shopping on company time. Some people may check sports scores when they're supposed to be balancing the corporate books. And a few people make occasional visits to naughty sites. Do you want your boss, spouse, or anyone else to be able to reconstruct your day — no matter whether it's innocuously off topic or more seriously inappropriate?

You can take three important steps to make sure that what happens on your laptop stays *off* your laptop:

✔ Make settings in your browser that limit the amount of information recorded.

✔ Use the browser's facilities to manually clean up the records on a regular basis.

✔ Employ a utility that performs a regular deep cleaning of temporary files, *URLs* (web sites) page histories, and *cookies* (tracking code placed on your hard drive by some Internet sites). Products from Symantec, McAfee, and other companies do the cleaning for you.

Start with the settings on your browser; I assume you're using the most common software, Microsoft Internet Explorer. Version 7 operates in a similar but slightly different manner than version 6.

1. Start your browser.

2. Click Tools➪Internet Options; see Figure 10-7.

3. Go to the General tab.

   You find five sections. Concentrate on the second setting: Browsing History.

4. Click the Delete button.

   Doing so gives you choices to remove Temporary Internet Files, Cookies, History, Form Data, and Passwords.

5. Click Close when you have finished removing all traces of your Internet experience.

6. Adjust the size of the Temporary Internet Files folder; see Figure 10-8.

   To adjust the size of the cache In Internet Explorer 7, go the General tab of the Internet Options dialog box and click the Settings button (under Browsing History).

**Figure 10-7**

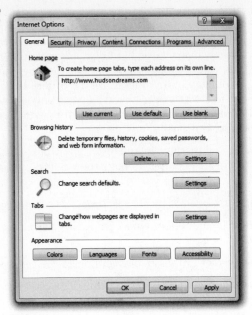

**Figure 10-8**

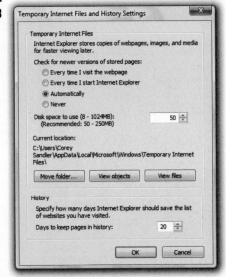

Doing so helps reduce the amount of information retained by your computer. This folder, like the Recycle Bin (in a logical sense), fills up from the bottom; each time a new file is stored, it displaces an older one that's reached the top. If you have a very large hard disk drive, you might be tempted to devote a large amount of space to this temporary folder. Doing so lets some web pages display more quickly; on the other hand, a smaller folder limits the size of the electronic trail you leave as you work on the Internet. (The XP and Vista versions are similar, but the Vista screen once again brings together more options in one place.)

You can have the system list the files in any order you want. To have them listed by file size, click the Size header; to have them listed by date, click the Last Modified, Last Accessed, or Last Checked header.

7. From the Settings page, click the View Files button.

    Look at the specific files being held in your computer's hard disk as the result of your Internet travels.

8. Click individual files or select groups of files and press the Delete key.

    By clicking one of the column headers in the listing, you can reorder the files by size, type, date created, date accessed, or other criteria. This allows you to search for particular files you want to remove from viewing. See Figure 10-9.

**Figure 10-9**

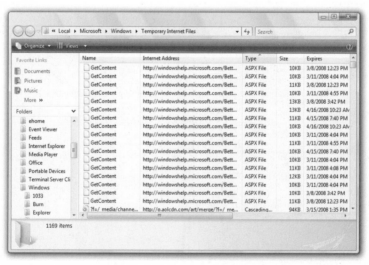

If you use the facilities of one of the advanced third-party programs such as Symantec's Norton SystemWorks or Norton 360 (shown in Figure 10-10), you can use tools that allow you to easily view all the downloaded bits of information, including web addresses, cookies, images, and videos. It brings together in one place all the displays you can find one by one from within Internet Explorer, and it adds some organizational niceties.

You can display the data by date or by the location name on your computer. Items can be individually cleaned or an entire group or folder can be stricken from the drive.

**Figure
10-10**

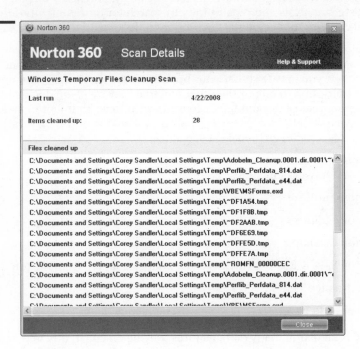

Note that no solution will absolutely guarantee that a law enforcement agency or a very determined expert who gains physical control over your laptop isn't going to be able to find some snippets and hints of your online travels. Remember that even when a file is "erased," it sits on the drive until a new file overwrites it.

But of course, in this book I'm talking about the reasonable expectation of privacy enjoyed by law-abiding citizens of the digital universe. The combination of these three steps should be sufficient to keep an honest user's machine and conscience clean.

# Sticking with Security and System Maintenance Utilities

I fully endorse the concept of belt and suspenders. Whenever possible, I encase my laptop within a cocoon of hardware, software, and human intelligence defenses. When my laptop is sitting alongside my desktop machine, both are plugged into a router that includes a hardware firewall to protect against most attempts against intrusion over the web. Both machines (and all the others in my office) run antivirus and adware detectors. Finally, I regularly use the facilities of a system analysis and repair utility to search for unwanted interference, intentional changes, or accidental corruption to the essential system files.

In my opinion, the two best product lines are those from McAfee (part of Network Associates) and Norton Utilities (from Symantec). I use both and recommend either; you may find that your broadband ISP may offer a free or discounted subscription to one or the other and that may help you decide between them. Other sources of discounted or free subscriptions: Your laptop maker may provide service with the machine, or your online banking portal may partner with one of the companies to make a special offer.

The key Norton products are Norton 360 or Norton SystemWorks. The Premier version of SystemWorks includes

- ✔ Norton AntiVirus
- ✔ Norton Utilities
- ✔ Norton Cleanup
- ✔ Norton Save & Restore (disk imaging utilities adapted from Norton Ghost)
- ✔ Performance Test
- ✔ Symantec Recovery Disk (creates an emergency boot CD)

Norton 360 is similar in many of its features, relying on constantly updated online components. The program in its version 2.0, released in 2008, includes

- ✔ PC Security
- ✔ Transaction Security (for online activities)
- ✔ PC Tuneup (see Figure 10-11)
- ✔ Access to a limited amount of online storage (which you can expand for more money) for backups of files and settings

**Figure 10-11**

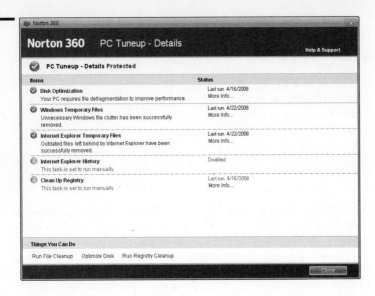

The Norton programs automatically block and remove virus, worm, and Trojan Horse infections, scanning both inbound and outbound e-mail and instant messaging attachments. Among their strengths are the ability to detect threats before they are run on the system; they check for specific viruses and worms from a regularly updated list and also are able to look for programs that produce suspicious behavior.

On the system checkup side, SystemWorks examines the Windows registry in search of malicious settings changes or accidental damage. An alternate product suite is Norton Internet Security, which combines Norton AntiVirus, Norton Personal Firewall, Norton Privacy Control, and Norton AntiSpam. There's a whole lot of protection in that package, minus the system repair utility.

# Part 11

# Keyboard Shortcuts for Laptop Users

Laptops, as you know, move about from place to place. And some of those places — like seatback tray tables on airlines or flimsy tables in hotel rooms — aren't anywhere nearly as comfortable workplaces as you have when you're at a proper desk. Add to the equation the fact that many road warriors use their laptops as the engines to put forth presentations in the boardroom, in an auditorium, or even in the living room.

In the early days of personal computing, everything was done from the keyboard: commands, selections, and settings. All that function still lies beneath Windows, and sometimes keyboard shortcuts come back to the future as conveniences.

## In this part . . .

- ✔ Working with laptop hot keys
- ✔ Putting symbols in text

# Dabbling in Laptop Hot Keys

Laptop designers can assign just about any task to one of the 12 function keys on a typical keyboard, or to one of the special-purpose buttons on particular models. I've presented here some typical assignments from current laptops from three major manufacturers: Hewlett-Packard (HP), IBM (now manufactured by and sold by a company called Lenovo), and Toshiba.

Some of the function keys aren't assigned to particular tasks on every model of every machine, and some manufacturers seem to take a perverse pleasure in using a scheme that's completely different from any other maker's. I've left the fifth column open; feel free to write in the assignments from your laptop. Neatness counts.

| Function Key | HP* | IBM* | Toshiba* | My Machine |
|---|---|---|---|---|
| Fn+F1 | Open Help and Support screen | — | Initiate security mode; blanks screen and goes to password log-in if enabled | |
| Fn+F2 | Open print window | — | Display power use window and allow mode selection | |
| Fn+F3 | Open default Internet browser | Turn off LCD display; press any key to turn on LCD | Initiate standby. Press power button to resume. | |
| Fn+F4 | Switch the image among displays | Initiate standby; press F4 to resume | Initiate hibernation. Press power button to resume. | |
| Fn+F5 | Initiate standby | — | Cycle through power-on display modes including LCD, external monitor, and multiple devices | |
| Fn+F6 | Initiate QuickLock** | — | Decrease screen brightness | |
| Fn+F7 | Decrease screen brightness | Switch between LCD and attached external monitor | Increase screen brightness | |

| Function Key | HP* | IBM* | Toshiba* | My Machine |
|---|---|---|---|---|
| Fn+F8 | Increase screen brightness | Turn screen expansion on or off | Enable/disable WiFi system | |
| Fn+F9 | Play, pause, or resume audio CD or DVD | — | Disable/enable touchpad | |
| Fn+F10 | Stop an audio CD or DVD | — | Turn cursor key overlay on or off | |
| Fn+F11 | Play the previous track or chapter in audio CD or DVD | — | Certain models: Turn numeric keypad overlay on/off | |
| Fn+F12 | Play the next track or chapter in audio CD or DVD | Turn on hibernation mode; to resume, press power button for <4 seconds | Certain models: Turn scroll lock on/off | |
| Fn+Esc | Display system information | — | Enable/disable volume mute | |
| Fn+PgUp | — | Turn ThinkLight on or off | — | |
| Fn+Home | — | Increase screen brightness | — | |
| Fn+End | — | Decrease screen brightness | — | |
| Fn+spacebar | — | Magnify desktop and maximize application windows | Magnify desktop and maximize application windows | |

*Sample machines HP Pavilion zt3001US, IBM ThinkPad A30, Toshiba Satellite M35X-S111, and Toshiba Satellite P205-S6287

**An HP security feature that disables the keyboard and goes to the log-on screen to await a password

# Inserting Symbols in Text

*For Dummies*®, as I'm sure you know, is a registered trademark of the publisher John Wiley & Sons, Inc. And this book is ©2008 by those same good folks.

But less well known to many users is the fastest way to get those symbols, the ® and the ©, not to mention ™, into the text of a file. Here are two ways, using Microsoft Word; the same principle applies in other programs that run under Windows.

## Using the mouse to insert symbols

It's amazing what people will register as trademarks. You never know when you'll need to insert a symbol.

1. Put the cursor where you want to add the symbol.

2. Take one of your hands off the keyboard and find the pointing device.

3. Click Insert⇨Symbols.

4. Click+drag down the Symbol chart slider until you see the ® symbol.

   Or, if you are using Word 2007, click the Symbol arrow.

5. Click the ® symbol to highlight it.

6. Choose an option:

   • Double-click the highlighted symbol.

   • Move the mouse and click the Insert button.

7. Close the Symbol chart.

8. Return your hand to the proper position on the keyboard and continue typing.

## Using the keyboard to insert symbols

So, now, tell me again how using a mouse is quicker and simpler than using the keyboard? The key, to pardon the pun, is to know the key combinations; they're not secret, but they're hidden. I'm revealing this one:

1. Put the cursor where you want to add the symbol.

2. Press Ctrl+Alt+R.

3. Find key combinations by going back to that Symbol chart.

   You can even get to the Symbol chart without using the mouse; press the Alt key, then the I key, then the S key.

You find two pages of information. One presents the full range of available characters for the current font; the Special Characters tab is behind it. If you see the symbol you want on the special page, look for a simple shortcut key combination like Ctrl+Alt+R for ®. Otherwise, look for the symbol on the full listing; when you find it, highlight it and then look for the preassigned shortcut key at the bottom of the table. For example, the keyboard shortcut for the ¼ symbol is Alt+0188.

The trick here is to use your laptop's numeric keypad to enter the character.

4. Press the Num Lock key.

5. Press the Alt key.

6. Type the number combination, using the numeric keypad.

7. Release the Alt key to earn your ¼.

Some characters are more complex to invoke than others. For example, some non-English characters require you to type an entire number first and then (without an intervening space) type a key combination like Alt+X.

Where's the Num Lock on a laptop? Well, you're going to have to find it for yourself, since the manufacturer could have placed it almost anywhere. On my newest machine, you turn on or off Num Lock by pressing the Fn key and then the F11 key. (An older machine uses F9.) Then use the numeric keypad, which is embedded in the keyboard amongst the characters on the right side. (My new machine even has a shortcut to the shortcut; I don't have to turn on and off the Num Lock. All I have to do is press Fn+Alt while typing numbers on the numeric keypad.)

Here are some of the more valuable special characters and their standard keyboard shortcuts. This assumes that you haven't changed the shortcuts by assigning them to a macro, something else you can do to speed the process. I've ordered them by function.

Monetary symbols appear in the following table.

| Symbol | Unicode / ASCII |
| --- | --- |
| € | Alt+0128 |
| ¢ | Alt+0162 |
| £ | Alt+0163 |
| ¥ | Alt+0165 |

Punctuation, typesetting, business, math, and accented characters follow in this table.

| Symbol | Unicode (Hex) | ASCII (Decimal) |
|---|---|---|
| ¡ | 00A1 followed by Alt+X | Alt+0161 |
| | Alt+Ctrl+! | |
| ¶ | 00B6 followed by Alt+X | Alt+0182 |
| ¿ | 00BF followed by Alt+X | Alt+0191 |
| | Alt+Ctrl+? | |
| ¹ | 00B9 followed by Alt+X | Alt+0185 |
| ² | 00B2 followed by Alt+X | Alt+0178 |
| ³ | 00B3 followed by Alt+X | Alt+0179 |
| © | 00A9 followed by Alt+X, or Alt+Ctrl+C | Alt+0169 |
| ® | 00AE followed by Alt+X, or Alt+Ctrl+R | Alt+0174 |
| ™ | 2122 followed by Alt+X, or Alt+Ctrl+T | Alt+0153 |
| ° | 02DA followed by Alt+X | Alt+0176 |
| ± | 00B1 followed by Alt+X | Alt+0177 |
| > | 03BC followed by Alt+X | Alt+0181 |
| ¼ | 00BC followed by Alt+X | Alt+0188 |
| ½ | 00BD followed by Alt+X | Alt+0189 |
| ¾ | 00BE followed by Alt+X | Alt+0190 |
| À | 00E0 followed by Alt+X | Alt+0224 |
| Á | 00E1 followed by Alt+X | Alt+0225 |
| Ç | 00E7 followed by Alt+X | Alt+0231 |
| È | 00E8 followed by Alt+X | Alt+0232 |
| É | 00E9 followed by Alt+X | Alt+0233 |
| Ê | 00EA followed by Alt+X | Alt+0234 |
| Û | 00FB followed by Alt+X | Alt+0251 |

# Using General Keyboard Shortcuts

Think retro: You can do almost everything from the keyboard that you can do with a mouse, including manipulate text. Here are some of the most useful commands.

Selecting, copying, and moving text may find you using these commands.

| Task | Shortcut |
|---|---|
| Select all | Ctrl+A |
| Select block of text | Shift+*arrow key* |
| Highlight a block of text | Ctrl+Shift+*arrow key* |
| Copy selected text or image to the Clipboard | Ctrl+C |
| Cut selected text or image | Ctrl+X |
| Paste selected text or image | Ctrl+V |
| Undo the previous action; some programs have multiple levels | Ctrl+Z |
| Redo the previous action | Ctrl+Y |
| Delete selected text or image | Delete |
| Delete selected item permanently, without placing the item in the Recycle Bin | Shift+Delete |
| Display the Help index | F1 |
| Rename the selected file | F2 |

Use the following commands when you need to move an insertion point.

| Task | Shortcut |
|---|---|
| Move the insertion point to the beginning of the next word | Ctrl+→ |
| Move the insertion point to the beginning of the previous word | Ctrl+← |
| Move the insertion point to the beginning of the next paragraph | Ctrl+↓ |
| Move the insertion point to the beginning of the previous paragraph | Ctrl+↑ |

When working with programs in open windows, you may find the following commands helpful.

| Task | Shortcut |
|---|---|
| Switch between open items | Alt+Tab |
| Switch to the previous open program | Alt+Shift+Tab |
| Cycle through items in the order they were opened | Alt+Esc |
| Cycle through programs on the taskbar using Windows 3-D (Windows Vista only) | ⊞+Tab |
| Open the shortcut menu for the active window | Alt+spacebar |
| Display the shortcut menu for the selected item | Shift+F10 |
| Display the System menu for the active window | Alt+spacebar |
| Display the Start menu | Ctrl+Esc or ⊞ |
| Display the corresponding drop-down menu | Alt+*underlined letter* |
| Perform a command from an open drop-down menu | *Underlined letter of a command name* |
| Open the next menu to the right, or open a submenu | → |
| Open the next menu to the left, or close a submenu | ← |

Windows commands follow here.

| Task | Shortcut |
|---|---|
| Search for a file or folder | F3 |
| View the properties for a selected object | Alt+Enter |
| Close the active item or quit the active program | Alt+F4 |
| Close the active document | Ctrl+F4 |
| Update (refresh) the active window | F5 |
| Cancel the current task | Esc |
| Open the Task Manager | Ctrl+Shift+Esc |
| Display the address bar list | F4 |
| Change the size of icons on the desktop | Ctrl+mouse scroll wheel movement |

Microsoft Internet Explorer commands follow in this table.

| Task | Shortcut |
|------|----------|
| Open the Organize Favorites dialog box | Ctrl+B |
| Open the Search bar | Ctrl+E |
| Start the Find utility | Ctrl+F |
| Open History | Ctrl+H |
| Open Favorites | Ctrl+I |
| Open the Open dialog box | Ctrl+L or Ctrl+O |
| Open another browser with the same web address | Ctrl+N |
| Open the Print dialog box | Ctrl+P |
| Update the current web page | Ctrl+R |
| Close the current window | Ctrl+W |

# Emergency Kit

When it comes to a device like a laptop, things happen. And things tend to happen at the worst possible time: at 30,000 feet over the Rockies or in a hotel room as you polish your presentation for the next morning. One thing you do have, of course, is this book. In this part, I offer some advice on dealing with things that go bump in the night or any other time of the day. You're not going to get any advice that involves soldering irons, writing computer code, or glue guns; this chapter's solutions are common sense.

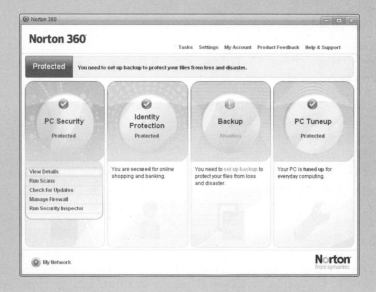

## In this part . . .

- ✓ **Finding the problem**
- ✓ **Working on common laptop troubles**

# *Looking for the Obvious and Obscure*

There aren't enough words in the dictionary to describe all the possible combinations of mechanical failures, human errors, and software bollixes that result in a laptop not computing.

However . . . in nearly 30 years in the personal computer industry, I'm pretty sure of at least Seven Most Likely Sources of Laptop Problems. Some of them are easy to fix, and some of them are extremely bad news.

But before you declare your laptop as dead as a Monty Python parrot ("stiff, bereft of life, resting in peace, off the twig, kicked the bucket, shuffled off its mortal coil, and a member of the choir invisible"), consider the Seven Most Likely Sources Of Laptop Problems.

## Lack of power

Powerlessness can come (or not come) from many sources.

### A problem with the battery

Consider these possibilities:

- ✔ **The battery may be fully discharged.** Even if a laptop computer is not being used, the battery will slowly drain over time; the older and more used the system, the shorter the shelf life for the battery.

- ✔ **The battery may be improperly installed in its slot or bay.** On one of my machines, there was an unfortunate design flaw that allowed the battery to work its way out of its connectors while traveling. (Once it even completely fell away from the laptop, staying behind on my desktop while I left town with the machine. I was reduced to using the machine only with the AC source.)

  Try running the machine from its AC adapter. If it comes to life, you know that the computer itself is working. The next task is to determine whether the battery was merely bereft of electrons and needs to be charged, or whether it can't hold a charge and needs to be replaced.

### A problem with the AC adapter

Consider these possibilities:

- ✔ **The AC adapter may be improperly connected.** Some adapters have two cords — one that plugs into the wall outlet at one end and the incoming side of the adapter at the other, and another cord that plugs into the adapter output and continues to a plug that connects to the laptop. Make certain everything is snugly attached. The wall outlet may not be live. Try another outlet, or plug a lamp or radio in to confirm that it's powered. Remember that some wall outlets are controlled by wall switches and may not be powered all the time. Many wall outlets in Europe (they call them *mains*) also have a small on/off switch right at the socket.

↙ **The laptop's internal electrical parts may have problems.** This isn't good news. The motherboard, the AC adapter, or another critical component is fried. If you can borrow a *compatible,* known-good AC adapter from a friend, repair shop, or store, see if it brings the computer to life. If not, decide whether the system is worth repairing.

## Wireless hardware

Nearly all current laptop computers with built-in WiFi circuitry have a physical switch that you must turn on to energize the transmitter/receiver. (The switch is there to help conserve battery power when the WiFi system isn't needed, and also to comply with requirements by airlines and some high-security offices that there be no unauthorized radio equipment in use.)

Consult your laptop's instruction manual or call the support desk to find the switch; better machines may add a tiny LED indicator that glows when power is on. Note that some machines may enable or disable the circuitry with a *soft switch* within a utility program; these systems may have *both* a physical and a soft switch.

The other common cause for WiFi problems is the lack of an acceptable signal or a blocked signal. Certain types of objects, including metal screens or particular types of building construction, block signals. And the fact is that some laptops have better antennae or better receivers; I've been in situations where the guy next to me can pick up a strong signal, while I get nothing. Sometimes the solution is to rotate the laptop or move to a new location.

## Wired hardware

A damaged or improperly attached Ethernet cable at the laptop or router end may be the culprit. Try substituting a known-good replacement cable.

Problems with the *network interface card (NIC)* may be the cause, too. If you're using an external adapter that connects to the laptop's USB port or PC Card slot, make sure it's properly plugged in. External devices usually have LED lights that indicate a proper connection; consult the instruction manual for the device to determine their precise meaning.

Under either operating system, once you get to the Network Adapters item, you will see a hardware report in the Device status window. If you want to continue searching for a hardware problem, click the Troubleshoot button and follow the instructions given by Windows.

Windows Vista users can check on the status of a built-in NIC in this way:

1. Click the Start button and choose Control Panel.

   If you're using the simplified view of available controls, go to Step 2. If not, go to Step 3.

2. Choose System and Maintenance⇨System⇨Device Manager.

   If you're using the Classic view, click Device Manager directly.

3. Expand the Network Adapters item.

4. Double-click the listed hardware.

Windows XP users can check on the status of a built-in NIC in this way:

1. Go to the Windows Control Panel and double-click the System icon.

2. Choose the Hardware tab and then click the Device Manager button.

3. Expand the Network Adapters item.

4. Double-click the listed hardware.

## Wireless software

Nearly all laptop manufacturers add special utility programs to the Control Panel to set up and manage the WiFi circuitry. A typical wireless link utility includes a Hardware tab that includes a report on the device status, properties, and a Troubleshoot button.

## Wired software

Windows Vista users have several ways to troubleshoot a network connection, including utilities from Microsoft as well as from laptop or other hardware manufacturers.

If your problem is apparent after you install new software, try the following:

1. Click the Start button and go to the Control Panel.

2. Choose Network and Internet⇨Network and Sharing Center.

3. Choose Manage Network Connections.

4. Right-click a listed connection.

5. Click Properties.

To run an automated and somewhat-capable diagnosis program under Vista, make certain all wires are properly connected and that the computer and any modems, routers, or other devices are turned on. Then do the following:

1. Right-click the network icon in the notification area at the bottom of the screen.

2. Open Network Diagnostics.

3. Choose Diagnose and Repair⇨Network and Sharing Center.

4. Choose Manage Network Connections.

5. Right-click a listed connection.

6. Click Properties.

Windows XP users can troubleshoot settings this way:

1. Go to the Control Panel.

2. Double-click the Network Connections icon.

3. Double-click the *local area network (LAN)* set up on your machine.

   • If no network is set up, then *there's your problem.* Go back to the Control Panel and this time choose Network Setup Wizard.

   • If you do have a LAN and double-click it, you go to the Local Area Connection Status window. Go to Step 4.

4. Choose the Support tab.

   You see a report from Windows about the connection and can click a Repair button (to attempt to fix problems) or refresh the settings.

## Virus warning or virus-like activity

Has your antivirus program intervened with a message? Did that message tell you it's detected a malicious or otherwise unwanted bit of code that either just arrived via e-mail or Internet, or one that's been activated and is attempting to take control? Follow carefully the instructions you see.

In most cases, a capable antivirus program offers to immediately delete the virus or place it in a safe, isolated location where it can do no harm. Once you've done that, follow these steps:

1. Shut down all open files and programs.

2. Go to the antivirus software's control panel.

3. Conduct a full system scan.

Depending on the size of your hard disk drive, this can take a few hours; don't put it off. An undetected virus can corrupt or destroy data and otherwise make your laptop computing experience miserable. And it could also spread to other machines on your network, and to the people in your e-mail address book.

Once you've cleaned up the mess, try to figure out how the virus got there in the first place. Is your antivirus program properly configured to protect against all threats? Are its definitions up to date?

Now about that "even worse" case: If you detect virus-like behavior on a laptop that doesn't have an antivirus program in place, take these steps:

1. Immediately shut down the machine to prevent further damage or mischief.

2. Get thee hence to a computer store and purchase a capable antivirus program.

   That program should include the ability to boot the system from its own disk (avoiding possibly infected Windows boot tracks).

   Several antivirus manufacturers offer Web-based utilities that alert you of a virus and may even remove the infection or stop its action. However, you still need to buy an antivirus program, and I recommend installing and running it with your computer disconnected from the Internet to prevent further infection or damage.

3. Load the antivirus program and follow all instructions.

4. Allow it to conduct a full scan to locate and remove viruses.

5. Load Windows and install the antivirus software on the disk.

6. Conduct another scan before using the machine.

## Unexplained slowdown and strange Internet behavior

You just might have a system that's clogged up with *adware* and *spyware,* which are unwanted snippets of programs that report on your Internet comings and goings to outsiders.

Although the makers of these programs may claim that their products are benign (they'll say they help deliver customized content to you when you visit the home pages of advertisers), many users feel otherwise. At best, they're an intrusion, and at worst they may deliver confidential information to thieves. And whether they're "good" or "bad," nearly all of them steal some of your computer's speed as they build up on the disk.

You can use the facilities of a capable system utility, such as Norton 360 or Norton SystemWorks (at www.symantec.com) or McAfee Security Center (at www.mcafee.com), to scour your Internet browser to remove *cookies* (records of visits and sign-ons) and other notations placed by advertisers. See Figure 12-1.

You can also use a specialized cleaner like Ad-Aware, which you can find in a free version (as well as a more capable commercial version) at www.lavasoft.com. (In my opinion, the advantage that products like AdAware had in recent years has mostly been eclipsed by utilities from the bigger players.)

**Figure 12-1**

 Clean your system at least once a month, and more often if you spend most of your time online.

## No video

Short and simple: Have you managed to shut off the LCD screen and redirect video output to the VGA, DVI, or S-Video output for an external monitor or television? Most laptops have a key combination that lets you use the LCD only, the LCD and an external monitor, or (and this one could be the problem) the external monitor only. Consult the machine's manual or study the keyboard itself to determine the keys; on some machines it's the Fn+F5 combination.

One other possibility is that your system BIOS has somehow been changed, perhaps as the result of an electrical shock, a system crash, or a virus. Check the instruction manual for the key to press during bootup to display the BIOS, and then look for the entry that refers to video output; it should say *LCD.*

## Defects onscreen

Laptops have two types of screen problems: those you can learn to live with, and those that require you to ship the machine to a repair shop for what may be costly surgery.

One or more thin, black or white, horizontal or vertical lines that run across the screen indicate developing problems with the LCD electronics. Usually this can be repaired; if still under warranty, the work may be done for free. Otherwise, expect a bill of a few hundred dollars, depending on the model. However, the image or text may still be readable and some users are willing to put up with the problem, which may never get worse. (Some manufacturers consider this an "acceptable" level of failure and don't include it in warranty coverage.)

A more serious problem is a dim or discolored display, which a technician has to deal with. And, of course, a completely dead screen has to be repaired.

You can, though, work around a failed screen by attaching an external computer monitor to the VGA or DVI output, or by using an S-Video or composite video output to a television set. (Consult your instruction manual for the keyboard combination to enable the external video output.)

If your laptop can deliver an image to an external monitor, you can continue using it that way — although it's a bit problematic to lug a 36" Sony onto an airline seat-back tray. But the mere fact that you can see an image on an external device is one way to determine if the problem is isolated to the screen or if it's a more complex, expensive problem caused by a motherboard or video circuitry failure.

## No sound of music

Two common problems cause a sudden end to music, system alerts, and other essential noises: The hardware volume wheel has rotated to 0 or the software volume control has been muted. The unfortunate thing is that both of these problems can sneak up on you unexpectedly.

On most laptops, the rotary volume control for built-in speakers is on the side of the machine; you can very easily move it one way or another as you slide your laptop into a carrying case. And for reasons that neither Microsoft nor any other support desk has ever adequately explained to me, the Windows volume control's mute buttons can easily be enabled accidentally in the course of ordinary computing. The same problem can also afflict a third-party software volume control associated with a separate sound card.

To fix the hardware thumbwheel, turn it up. To fix the software mute, choose one of the following sets of steps:

**Option 1:**

1. Double-click the volume control icon that may appear in the system tray or the taskbar.

2. Look for the checkboxes next to the Mute option for the various available services:

    • Wave/MP3: For most users, for music playback and games.

    • CD Audio: You can figure this one out on your own, right?

- MIDI: Controls certain digital musical instruments.

- TAD-In: Less common on laptops, this audio service is used with computer-attached *telephone answering devices (TADs)*.

3. Remove the checkmark for any service you want to use.

4. Ensure the master volume control and mute that shuts off all sound card output are deselected.

 The master volume control should generally be set to its highest level, allowing fine-tuning using the hardware thumbwheel.

**Option 2:**

1. Open the Control Panel and double-click Sounds and Audio Devices Properties.

 Most hardware components customize the Windows control here.

2. Ensure the master Mute checkbox is deselected.

 The master volume control should generally be set to its highest level, allowing fine-tuning using the hardware thumbwheel.

## *Recording the News You Can Use*

Before you hit the road, take the time to write down some of the most important details about your laptop, just in case.

Just in case

- ✔ Your laptop is stolen, misplaced, or otherwise absent. You'll need details to file a police or insurance report or to reclaim it from lost and found.

- ✔ Your laptop gives up the ghost and you need to contact the support desk for assistance or to arrange for repair.

- ✔ You need to contact the maker of the operating system or major software to deal with a problem.

Here's a little list. I suggest you keep the information separate from your laptop; if you bring this book along with you while you travel, you might want to make a copy of this section and place the information in a suitcase, not your laptop case.

| *Hardware* | *My Information* |
|---|---|
| Laptop manufacturer* | |
| Model name* | |
| Model number* | |
| Serial number* | |
| Installed RAM | MB or GB |
| Hard drive capacity | GB |
| Operating system and version | |
| Operating system product key* | |
| My laptop's BIOS Setup is accessed by pressing this key while the operating system is starting | |
| Modifications I've made to the original hardware | |

*Look on the underside of the machine for a sticker with this information and more.

| *Support and Warranty* | *My Information* |
|---|---|
| Purchase date | |
| Store or online dealer name | |
| Order number or sales receipt number | |
| Dealer's customer service phone number | |
| Length of manufacturer warranty | |
| Length of extended warranty | |
| Manufacturer's technical support telephone | |
| Manufacturer's technical support web site | |

| *Major Software Installed* | *My Information* |
|---|---|
| Office suite product name and version number | |
| Location of original disks and serial number | |
| Support web site and phone number | |
| Graphics software product name and version number | |

| Major Software Installed | My Information |
|---|---|
| Location of original disks and serial number | |
| Support web site and phone number | |
| Video and audio editor/playback software and version number | |
| Location of original disks and serial number | |
| Support web site and phone number | |

| Internet and E-mail | My Information |
|---|---|
| Internet service provider (ISP) | |
| Internet login/sign-on name** | |
| ISP technical support phone | |
| ISP technical support web site | |
| My primary e-mail address** | |
| My secondary e-mail address** | |

**Don't write down your passwords in the same place as your login name.

Manufacturer emergency contact numbers should be handy at all times.

| Manufacturer | Phone | Web |
|---|---|---|
| Acer | 800-816-2237 | www.acerpanam.com |
| Compaq | 800-652-6672 | www.hp.com/country/us/en |
| Dell | 888-560-8324 | http://support.dell.com |
| Fujitsu | 800-838-5487 | http://support.fujitsupc.com/CS/Portal/supporthome.do |
| Gateway | Gateway direct: 800-846-2301; Retail products: 408-273-0808 | http://support.gateway.com |
| Hewlett-Packard | 800-474-6836 | www.hp.com/country/us/en |
| Lenovo (IBM) | 800-426-7378 | www.lenovo.com/think/us/en/ |
| Sony | 888-476-6972 | http://esupport.sony.com |

Major ISPs can be reached at these numbers.

| ISP | URL | Phone |
| --- | --- | --- |
| AOL | www.aol.com | 800-827-6364 |
| Boingo WiFi | www.boingo.com | 800-880-4117 |
| Comcast | www.comcast.com | 866-886-6838 |
| Cox | www.cox.com | Varies by area |
| EarthLink (dial-up) | www.earthlink.net | 888-327-8454 |
| Sprint PCS WiFi | www1.sprintpcs.com | 866-727-9434 |
| T-Mobile Hot Spots | http://hotspot.t-mobile.com | 800-866-2453 |

# Troubleshooting the Common Cold Computer

The basic rules of troubleshooting, or at least my basic rules, are based on the following steps.

## The laptop hasn't ever worked

If it hasn't, you need to either return the machine to its maker or seller, or work with them to get it to perform as advertised. I'm talking here about a machine that's either dead on arrival or seriously misconfigured by the maker. In my book (which this is) it's the seller's responsibility to make sure it works properly before you get the chance to screw it up.

## New hardware or software is misbehaving

If your laptop gets wonky after an installation, you don't have to be a rocket scientist to pinpoint the new device or program as the problem. Your goal should be to first undo whatever damage you may have done to the settings or machine configuration. Once that's done, and the laptop is working the way it was before, try a careful reinstallation. Make only one change at a time — don't install two pieces of software, or two new devices — before testing the machine. By putting in one piece at a time, you should be able to determine if one of them is the source of the problem.

## The laptop suddenly stops working properly

You have a number of options if this is the case:

- **Virus or malware:** A virus or other form of malware may have insinuated itself onto the machine, corrupting or altering settings or issuing nasty commands. This shouldn't happen: Every laptop should be protected by a capable and regularly updated antivirus program, and every laptop user should know better than to run any program or open any e-mail attachment that arrives from an unknown or untrustworthy source.

If you suspect a virus, command your antivirus program to conduct a scan of the entire computer and follow its instructions for the removal of anything nasty it finds.

If you suspect a virus and your machine isn't protected by an antivirus program, shut it off. Then go to a computer store and purchase a capable antivirus program. Make sure you buy one capable of booting the system from its own installation disc, so it can work without allowing existing viruses to continue causing problems. Before installing the new program, disconnect the laptop from a wired Internet connection or shut off the wireless system before conducting the initial scan; then attach to the Internet for updates to the program and for additional scans.

✔ **Electrical anomaly:** This is less likely on a laptop computer (which operates from a stable, low-voltage battery or on the regulated DC side of an AC adapter) than on a desktop machine powered by sometimes- fluctuating AC power. You can use the Windows Restore facility (part of Windows Vista or XP) to go back to a day when the machine and its settings were copasetic. Similar functions can be found in some system utility programs, like Norton SystemWorks and Norton 360.

✔ **Component failure or disconnection:** This is, thankfully, relatively uncommon. The motherboard, memory, and microprocessor generally last for years. The parts of the laptop subject to failure include the following:

- Battery: Typically lasts for three or four years or something like 300 charge and discharge cycles. Usually the battery fails gradually. You'll notice it losing its charge more quickly or not holding as many hours of power. If the machine works properly when its AC adapter is attached, the problem lies with the battery.

- Keyboard or pointing device: These mechanical devices can fail over time. If you suspect a failure, try attaching an external keyboard or mouse.

- Power connectors or ports: On some machines, there are mechanical frailties, otherwise known as "accidents waiting to happen."

Be very careful working with a laptop whose power connector or other attachment is somewhere a push can cause it to snap off or bend. Another problem on some machines is the cabling between the motherboard and the LCD; don't overextend the angle you open your machine's top cover.

If the machine's running, even improperly, go to the Control Panel and choose the Device Manager. Look for exclamation points on the list that indicate a hardware failure or a problem with a device driver that enables them. Follow the troubleshooting instructions listed for each piece of hardware.

## Computer user, diagnose thyself

Many laptop manufacturers deliver their machines with a diagnostic program installed. You can also purchase a program and install it yourself. Follow the software maker's instructions to initiate the diagnostic and take full advantage of its facilities. If your machine is experiencing *intermittent* problems — occasional failures or errors that you can't reproduce on demand — instruct the diagnostic software to make multiple rounds of tests. In some situations, you may need to run the tests all night in hopes of catching an elusive bug.

Most diagnostic programs offer these test types:

- **Quick or express test:** Puts the machine through its basic paces; that's a good place to start.

- **Hard drive scan:** A more extended test. Can take an hour or more.

- **Custom test:** Can zero in on a particular set of components that you may suspect to be at fault.

## Computer user, let the Help desk inside

Some computer manufacturers use Windows or third-party facilities that allow them to give your machine a checkup over the Internet. This may be a good solution for some users, allowing a capable technician to analyze your system, change settings and configurations, or walk you through those changes yourself.

In theory, though, you're opening up your machine and all of its passwords and private information to an outsider. Although I'd like to think you can trust a professional not to go places that are inappropriate for the task, I'd rather be very safe than very sorry. Make sure you keep this in mind and be prepared to change passwords once the machine is back up and running.

## Disk drive blues

Disk drives fail sooner or later. If you're lucky, the drive continues working throughout the useful life of the machine; if you're less than lucky, or if the machine suffers a fall or other insult, the drive may come to an untimely demise.

The best way to proceed: Always assume that your hard drive will fail the next time you try to use it. By that I mean, make sure that you have backups of irreplaceable data on another medium: recordable CD or DVD, external hard drive, flash memory key, or another computer connected by a wired or wireless network or the Internet.

Once you're protected in that way, purchase and use a capable disk drive utility such as Diskkeeper or Norton SystemWorks or Norton 360. These programs can help efficiently maintain files, and should alert you to glitches before they become fatal problems — enough time to offload your essential data.

## Your machine's trying to tell you something

As annoying as they are, error messages generated by Windows can sometimes help you fix problems. Don't just curse at them; read them and make notes on what they say.

In some cases, error messages are just an occasional thing, something that pops up only with certain combinations of programs, commands, or keystrokes. In other situations, they may be reporting a serious problem that must be resolved before the machine is usable.

With your notes in hand, you can take several approaches:

 ✔ Search the Microsoft Knowledge Base (www.microsoft.com) for information and troubleshooting tips directly associated with the error message.

 ✔ Use an Internet search engine to see if user groups or individuals have posted information about the error.

 ✔ Call or e-mail your machine's support department and ask for assistance with the specific error code.

## Memory loss

If your machine reports insufficient memory to accomplish its tasks, the problem may be just that: not enough memory installed for certain sophisticated and demanding applications or for a particular set of programs running at the same time.

Before you purchase new memory, though, try shutting down the machine and restarting. Some insufficient memory messages are caused by very unusual sets of circumstances and may not recur for some time.

If you suspect a problem with your machine's memory, run a diagnostics program to test the modules. A module in a laptop may have become partly dislodged; consult the instruction manual for advice on how to reset them in place.

## Checking a driver

*Drivers* sit between your computer's hardware and its operating system, identifying and enabling each component's unusual features. When a piece of hardware stops working or acts in a nonstandard fashion, one of the first things to check is if its driver has become corrupted, erased, or made unusable because of other changes you made, such as updating your operating system.

The easiest way to check for driver problems is here:

*1.* Go to the Windows Control Panel ⇨ System and Maintenance ⇨ System.

*2.* Click Device Manager.

*3.* Scroll down the list and look for a yellow exclamation point.

This indicates a problem. If you find a yellow warning, the solution may be to reinstall the previous driver or install a new one.

## Reinstalling a driver

To reinstall a driver, follow these steps:

*1.* Double-click the device with the warning.

*2.* Click the Driver tab.

*3.* Click Update Driver.

Windows should list all the available drivers for the hardware, and that's often an acceptable way to fix the problem. If you have an updated version of the driver in a specific location, you can specify that to the system.

## Rolling back a driver

If the driver problem arises after you've installed a new driver, the first thing to do is see if the issue goes away by rolling back the system to a previous state:

*1.* From the Device Manager, right-click the problematic device.

*2.* Click Properties.

*3.* Click the Drivers tab.

*4.* Click Roll Back Driver.

## Using System Restore on a driver

If rolling back the driver doesn't solve the problem, use System Restore to return your computer to the way it was before you installed the new driver. Consult the web site or call the hardware's support desk to see if the manufacturer has a new driver or specific advice on dealing with problems.

## Soundless, pictureless CD or DVD

CDs and DVDs are wondrous expansions of laptops, but they're also very demanding of system resources and can sometimes fail. Try these tried-and-true troubleshooting steps:

✔ Ensure that the CD or DVD is properly mounted on the spindle.

✔ Test the drive. Insert another CD or DVD that has previously worked (or a commercially produced disc). If your laptop can see and use that disc, then you can assume that the drive is functioning and that the original disc was flawed or blank.

✔ See if Windows recognizes a working drive. Click the Start button, and then Computer (Windows Vista) or My Computer (Windows XP). If you don't see the CD or DVD drive listed as an available device, it or its driver may have a hardware problem. If so, go to the Control Panel, double-click the System icon, choose the Hardware tab, and check the drive status; follow the steps in the troubleshooting option.

✔ If you're having trouble writing data to a recordable CD or DVD, a number of sources may be the problem:

  • Verify that you're using the correct type of media. A CD-R drive can only use that sort of disc. A CD-RW can use either a CD-R or CD-RW disc. The various forms of writable DVDs have different requirements; the newest optical design, Blu-ray, generally works with most of the previous DVD and CD designs.

  • The drive may be unable to receive a steady data stream. Try closing all unnecessary programs before writing to the drive. You can also try reducing the write speed.

  • Turn off Standby mode in Windows to prevent the system from going into suspension because of lack of activity from the keyboard or mouse.

# Glossary: Tech Talk

**access time:** The amount of time needed to locate and then read or write data from or to a storage device, including disk drives and RAM. The access speed of memory chips is usually in the range of 10 to 150 nanoseconds; a nanosecond is a billionth of a second. Hard disks, which are mechanical devices, typically require about 8 to 15 milliseconds; a millisecond is a thousandth of a second. Less is better.

**All Programs menu:** In Windows, the full listing of installed programs and applications available to the system. Access it by clicking the Start icon, then the All Programs command. You can also reach it by pressing the Windows key and then clicking the All Programs command.

**Alt:** Another level of shift for the keyboard. Pressing the Alt key, together with a character or number from the numeric keyboard, results in transmission of a special character or command.

**analog:** A means of recording values by use of the fall and rise of a continuously variable signal. Standard voice communication over a telephone line uses an analog signal. By contrast, *digital* signals represent values with numbers that are translated to sounds, characters, colors, or brightness levels.

**application:** A software program that helps the user perform a specific function, such as word processing or spreadsheet analysis.

**ASCII code:** American Standard Code for Information Interchange. A definition that represents characters as numbers. The keyboard automatically generates codes for standard characters. Special characters can be created by using by using the Alt key as a shift and the numeric keypad. As an example, Alt+0174 yields the • character.

**aspect ratio:** A relationship calculated by dividing the width of an image or a laptop's screen by its height. The original aspect ratio for most computer monitors was 4:3. Many current laptops offer widescreen displays.

**bandwidth:** The amount of data that can be transmitted over an electronic line in a particular period of time. For digital devices, bandwidth is usually measured in bits per second or bytes per second. For analog devices, bandwidth is stated as the number of cycles per second, or Hertz (Hz). More is better.

**BD:** *See* Blu-ray.

**binary:** A base-two numbering system used by computers. All numbers are composed of 0s and 1s, representing either off (0) or on (1) or strung together as computer words that are read from right to left as powers of two.

**BIOS:** Basic Input/Output System. This is code, recorded on a special type of memory chip that does not require electrical power to hold its memory, that controls the lowest, most basic functions of the laptop. When the computer is first turned on, the BIOS helps *boot* the machine, loading the operating system. Once it is running, the BIOS acts as the interface between the hardware and the operating system, receiving and interpreting keystrokes and mouse clips and sending commands to the hard disk for access to data.

**bit:** A binary digit, the smallest piece of information in a computer, a single 0 or 1. A single bit can represent a number, ON or OFF, or TRUE or FALSE.

**bits per second:** bps. The number of binary digits transmitted or moved from place to place in one second.

**Blu-ray:** An advanced form of optical storage capable of holding as much as 25GB of data on a single-sided disc or 50GB on double-sided media. Blu-ray discs (sometimes referred to as BD) have the same physical dimensions as a standard DVD or CD, and store high-definition movies and other data.

**boot:** When your laptop is first turned on it must boot itself to life, configuring memory and loading the operating system. (The phrase comes from "lifting yourself up by your own bootstraps.") When you turn on the computer, the system performs a *hard boot* that includes *initializing* all the hardware. If you press Ctrl+Alt+Del, the computer performs a *soft boot,* which merely reloads the operating system.

**broadband:** A broadband communications medium can simultaneously carry multiple channels at high speeds. Think of your cable television system which techies call a "fat pipe" capable of delivering hundreds of channels as well as high-speed Internet and even telephone communication. The most common broadband technologies include cable, fiber optic, and DSL systems.

**burn:** A recordable optical device, such as a CD-R or DVD-R or the read/write versions of these storage systems, uses a laser to *burn* dark spots or pits in a disc that represents 1s or 0s of binary information.

**byte:** Eight bits, the smallest unit of data stored or moved in a laptop.

**cable modem:** A device that sends and receives data signals over a broadband cable television connection. It serves as the interface for Internet as well as VoIP (Voice over Internet Protocol) telephone service.

**CD-R:** Compact Disc-Recordable. An optical storage device that can write a permanent record to a special type of CD, which can then be read on a standard CD-ROM drive or another CD-R device.

**CD-ROM:** Compact Disc Read-Only Memory. This is the original read-only version of the CD, an adaptation of technology developed for the music recording industry. A CD-ROM can hold as much as 800MB of data.

**CD-RW:** Compact Disc-Rewritable. An optical storage device that can read, write, and rewrite information on a special type of CD.

**clipboard:** Under Windows, a block of data (including words, numbers, and images) can be temporarily copied to memory and later *pasted* into another open file. While it is in memory, it is considered held in the *clipboard.* If Windows is shut down or the power is turned off, the contents of the clipboard are lost unless you save it to disk.

**connector:** The end of a cable that plugs into a port usually terminates in a connector. A *male connector* has one or more exposed pins; a *female connector* has one or more openings that mate with pins on the port.

**Control Panel:** The central repository for utilities to make settings, configurations, and customizations of most of the features of the hardware and the operating system of your laptop. You can reach the Control Panel in a number of ways, including pressing the Start button and selecting it from available options; you can also reach the same display by pressing the Windows key from the keyboard.

**CPU:** The *Central Processing Unit* is an old-school term for microprocessor. *See also* microprocessor.

**Ctrl:** Another level of shift for the keyboard. Holding down the Ctrl key together with a character or number from the numeric keyboard will result in transmission of a special character or command.

**cursor:** A blinking or colored symbol that appears onscreen to indicate where the next character will appear. The cursor can be moved from the keyboard arrow keys or by clicking at a different place with the mouse. A second cursor, sometimes called a *pointer*, is controlled by the mouse or other pointing device and is used to select text or icons for action or to reposition the text cursor.

**default:** A predefined basic or standard value or setting for a program or the operating system. When you first configure hardware or software, you begin from the default setting; if your system runs into problems, you may want to take advantage of the opportunity to reset it to its default configuration.

**device driver:** A set of instructions that, in logical terms, sits between the BIOS and the operating system to identify the particular pieces of hardware installed in your laptop. Windows already knows how to work with a CD-R or a WiFi adapter, for example, but needs to know the particular details of the brand and model of device in your machine.

**disc, disk:** A spinning storage medium. A hard disk (notice the spelling style with a *k*) uses a platter that can hold magnetically encoded information. A CD or DVD disc (with a *c*) uses dark spots or pits that are read by a laser.

**double-click:** Windows distinguishes between a mouse click and a rapid double-click to select or perform an action. From the Windows Control Panel you can adjust the amount of time that is allowed to elapse between a pair of clicks to distinguish between a single- and double-click.

**drag:** To drag a block of text, an image, or an icon (including a folder), click it and keep the left mouse button held down while you move the onscreen pointer. When it is in the place where you want to *drop* the material, release the button.

**DSL:** A digital subscriber line is a special telephone connection for high-speed data communication. It is generally only usable at locations that are within a few miles of a phone company switching office where the information is transferred to higher-capacity cabling than the one that reaches to the home or office.

**dual-core:** *See* multicore.

**DVD:** A higher capacity evolution of the CD, capable of holding as much as 4.7GB of data in current single-sided devices with double-sided devices making their way to market. DVD originally stood for *digital video disc* and then *digital versatile disc* but today is rarely called anything but its initials.

**eSATA:** An extension of the Serial ATA input/output specification to allow attachment of external devices including hard disk drives and optical storage. *See also* SATA.

**Ethernet:** The most common design for local area networks used by personal computers and laptops. You'll likely find *10Base-T*, which permits data transfer rates of 10 Mbps and *100Base-T*, which allows transfer rates of 100 Mbps. A 10Base-T component on a 100Base-T network will operate at 10 MBps; a 100Base-T component on a 10Base-T network will also be limited to that lower speed.

**ExpressCard:** A means to add certain functions to a laptop through plugging in a small circuit card. An improvement to the PC Card or PCMCIA slot offered on early laptops. *See also* PC Card.

**file:** A collection of data that can represent words, numbers, sounds, images, or settings that is stored under a name.

**firewall:** A software or hardware device designed to block unauthorized intruders from gaining entry to an individual computer or a network.

**FireWire:** Apple's name for the IEEE 1394 high-speed serial communication specification; it is also called iLink in its implementation by Sony. It is similar to USB in its speed and flexibility. Most current laptops offer USB, while a smaller number also offer FireWire, mostly for use in connection with some digital camcorders and cameras.

**Fn key:** *See* function keys.

**font:** A collection of characters and symbols of a particular design for display on screen and in print. On a computer, a character set also carries a point size and other attributes such as **bold,** *italic,* and underline. In print, a 72-point character is about 1 inch tall; a 12-point font is about ⅙ inch high.

**function keys:** An extra set of keys on a computer keyboard, usually labeled F1 through F12, that can be programmed to perform special functions. Instruction manuals and help screens usually refer to them as *Fn* as in *Fn10* for the F10 key.

**gigabyte:** Technically, a gigabyte is 1,024 megabytes, or 1,073,741,824 bytes. Informally, it is used to refer to one billion bytes. Abbreviated as GB.

**HTML:** Hypertext Markup Language. The basic computer language used to lay out most Internet Web sites. Your browser interprets the HTML language and displays an onscreen image that uses available fonts, colors, and screen capabilities.

**hub:** A connection or splitting point for attached components including network cables, USB or FireWire devices, and other equipment. The hub can be *active* (with some intelligence to manage its activities), *passive,* and *powered* (providing electrical current to devices), or *unpowered.*

**icon:** A drawing or picture that represents an object or program. The object can be moved, copied, or deleted. If it's a program, clicking or double-clicking the icon can launch the application or a specific action.

**IEEE 1394:** A technical standard for high-speed serial communications marketed under its own name, as well as FireWire and iLink. *See also* FireWire.

**IP address:** An identifying number for devices on the Internet and many office networks.

**K:** Kilo. Technically, one kilobyte is actually 1,024 bytes, but marketers use a shorthand (and shortchange) of 1,000.

**Kb:** Kilobit. Technically, 1,024 bits. In practice, it often refers to 1,000 bits.

**KB:** Kilobyte. Technically, 1,024 bytes. Often used to mean 1,000 bytes.

**Kbps:** Kilobits per second.

**KBps:** Kilobytes per second.

**LCD:** Liquid Crystal Display. A display used on most laptops that produces images by changing the polarity of light passing through individual pixels in response to an electrical signal.

**malware:** Software or snippets of code inserted into e-mail, programs, or pictures that make your laptop do things you don't want it to. Can range from viruses to snooping programs.

**Mb:** *See* megabit.

**MB:** *See* megabyte.

**Mbps:** Megabits per second.

**MBps:** Megabytes per second.

**megabit:** Mb. Technically, 1,048,576 bits, but in practice often used to mean 1,000,000 bits.

**megabyte:** MB. Technically, 1,048,576 bytes, but in practice often used to mean 1,000,000 bytes.

**memory:** A computer's working space, the temporary resting place for data. Compare to storage, which is a record of information stored on disk or other media. In general, memory contents are erased when the computer's power is turned off.

**menu:** A selection of commands or options presented by the operating system or an application.

**microprocessor:** The essential chip that executes instructions and manipulates information in a computer. Current laptops generally use Intel chips, including those in the Pentium 4, Centrino, and Celeron families, or competitive chips from AMD, including the Athlon and Sempron families.

**modem:** Modulator/demodulator. In its original definition, the device that converts digital data from a computer into analog data for transmission over telephone lines by modulating it into waves. At the other end, a modem converts the analog data back into digital form by demodulating it. Cable modems also convert data, but that information may stay in digital form.

**multicore:** A CPU that combines two or more independent cores into a single package. A dual-core processor includes two cores and a quad-core processor contains four cores. Multicore processors can generally handle multitasking better than single-core CPUs.

**multitasking:** The ability of a CPU to perform more than one assignment at the same time, or to switch back and forth between tasks so fast that it delivers the functional equivalence of multiple tasking.

**operating system:** OS. The program that manages the computer's hardware and interfaces with the software applications. The most common OS on early PCs was DOS; today, nearly all desktop and laptop computers run a version of Microsoft Windows. Apple devices run an OS from that company.

**parallel:** A means of transmitting data with the bits that make up a computer word traveling alongside each other on adjacent wires, like the lanes of a superhighway. Until the arrival of the USB port, this was the most common means of communication with printers and some other devices. Compare to *serial*.

**parallel port:** The input/output channel to a parallel device.

**PC Card:** A credit-card-sized expansion device that plugs into a socket on many laptops. Type II cards are principally used for memory, network adapters, and modems. Type III cards were originally envisioned to hold miniaturized disk drives but that function has mostly been taken over by flash memory keys that plug into the USB port. The original name for these devices bore the forgettable acronym of PCMCIA. The original Type I card, thin and limited, is not commonly used in laptops. *See also* ExpressCard.

**PCMCIA:** *See* ExpressCard or PC Card.

**peer-to-peer:** A type of network in which any device can be the information source (server) or the information recipient (client). Ethernet is generally set up as a peer-to-peer network.

**phishing:** A scurrilous attempt by someone to obtain personal or financial information about others through the use of fraudulent or misleading e-mails or web sites.

**pointer:** *See* cursor.

**quad-core:** *See* multicore.

**RAM:** Random Access Memory. The working space of your laptop, used for the temporary resting place for work in progress and other purposes. Files must be saved to storage on hard disks or other media.

**read/write head:** On many types of storage device, this component reads recorded data and writes new information. Hard drives, floppy drives, and tape backup devices use magnetism to read and write; CD-Rs, CD-RWs, and DVD-RAMs use a laser to melt dark spots or pits on a plastic disc.

**router:** A device that bridges two or more networks together. The connection can link two Ethernets, for example, or one Ethernet and a shared connection to the Internet. Many routers include a firewall to block unwanted intruders.

**SATA:** A current standard to connect computers to storage devices such as hard drives and DVD drives using serial communication over thin cables. This simplifies the design of laptop cases and air circulation within them. *See also* eSATA.

**screen:** An LCD or television-like monitor that displays information from a computer.

**serial communications:** The transmission of information between devices, one bit at a time, over a single line. The most common current implementations of serial communication are USB and, to a lesser extent, FireWire.

**serial port:** A connector on a computer for a serial device. In practice, this refers to an old-style DB9 port. Today, the original serial communication hardware and protocol has been mostly replaced by the faster and more flexible Universal Serial Port.

**spam:** Unsolicited and usually unwanted e-mail sent by persons or companies who really think you are gullible enough to buy pharmaceuticals, "real" replicas of watches or handbags, or almost anything else. *See also* phishing.

**touchpad:** A touch-sensitive section of a laptop keyboard that can be used as a pointing device with accompanying left and right buttons.

**USB:** Universal Serial Bus. A high-speed, flexible communications method that can connect just about anything to a laptop; most new printers, scanners, and external modems and WiFi adapters use this port. The current version of the standard, 2.0, permits data transfer rates of as much as 12 Mbps, and a single port can connect as many as 127 devices.

**virus:** A piece of malware that spreads from machine to machine through e-mail or interchange of music, graphics, or program files.

**webcam:** A video camera (built into or connected to a laptop) that can send live (streaming) video or record video files that can be sent over the Internet.

**WiFi:** The general term for wireless networking. A WiFi system can be used to connect laptops and computers in a local area, to communicate with local printers and other devices, or to connect to a network that is linked to a shared broadband modem that links to the Internet.

**word:** The standard size for a chunk of data manipulated by the CPU. For 16-bit computers — the most common current design — a word is made up of two bytes. For 32-bit computers, a word is made up of four bytes.

**worm:** A form of virus or malware, a worm is a self-replicating computer program. It uses the Internet or a local area network (LAN) to send copies of itself to other systems. The worm may cause damage to files or merely slow down or halt computer communication or processing.

# Index

**Q**

**R**

**S**

# Notes

# Notes

# Notes

# Notes